AFTER THE TREES

AFTER THE TREES
Living on the
Transamazon Highway

Douglas Ian Stewart

UNIVERSITY OF TEXAS PRESS
AUSTIN

Requests for permission to reproduce material from this work should
be sent to Permissions, University of Texas Press, Box 7819,
Austin, TX 78713-7819.

♾ The paper used in this publication meets the minimum
requirements of American National Standard for Information
Sciences—Permanance of Paper for Printed Library Materials,
ANSI Z39.48-1984.

Library of Congress Cataloging-in-Publication Data

Stewart, Douglas Ian, 1968–
    After the trees : living on the Transamazon Highway / Douglas
Ian Stewart. — 1st ed.
        p.   cm.
    Includes bibliographical references and index.
    ISBN 0-292-77678-0 (alk. paper). — ISBN 0-292-77680-2
    (pbk. : alk. paper)
    1. Farms, Small—Amazon River Region.   2. Farms, Small—
Brazil.   3. Deforestation—Amazon River Region.
4. Deforestation—Brazil.   I. Title.
HD1476.A55S74   1994
338.1′6—dc20   93-49553

Bemvindo *means welcome in Portuguese.*
This is to my Amazonian family.

And to my mom, for her support, strength, and wisdom.

Bemvindo significa welcome *em Português.*
O livro é dedicado a minha familia Amazônica: Giovani, Floripse,
e Geraldo. Pelo bemvindo que me deram, obrigado.

E a minha mai, por seu apoio, fortitude, e heroismo.

CONTENTS

CONVENTIONS AND ACRONYMS USED IN THE TEXT

Forest peoples: includes both Native Americans and non-native peoples who live primarily from extractive industries like rubber tapping, fishing, and hunting. Forest peoples farm mainly for subsistence.

Colonists: *colonos* in Portuguese—family farmers on the frontier who migrated from other regions of the country.

Hectare: an area 100 meters by 100 meters, or about 2.4 acres.

Small farmers: colonists who own a single 100-hectare lot.

Medium farmers: colonists who own 200 to 500 hectares.

Large farmers: those who own more than 500 hectares. These might be referred to as *glebistas*, Portuguese for owners of *glebas* or large ranches. They are not usually referred to as *colonos* and are not included in the term *colonists* used herein.

Brazilian Acronyms Used in Text

CEPLAC: the government's Comissão Executiva do Plano de Lavoura Cacaueira (Executive Planning Commission for Cacao Production).

CIRA: Cooperativa Integral da Reforma Agraria (United Cooperative of the Agrarian Reform). At Km. 90, the CIRA was formed in the mid-1970s by the government. It dissolved during the mill crisis but was reorganized under colonist initiative in 1986.

Conan: company that bought PACAL in 1981 and went bankrupt in 1982.

COOPERFRON: Cooperative of the New Frontier. The strongest and broadest-based cooperative in the Altamira region in the 1970s. It could not get funding and fell apart in the 1980s.

DISPAM: Amazonian distributor. Sells cacao to the multinational Nestlé Corporation in São Paulo. Controls 90 percent of the Transamazonian cacao market.

EMATER: Empreza de Assistência Técnica e Extensão Rural (Agency for Technical Assistance and Rural Extension). Formerly ACAR: Associação Credito e Assistencia Rural (Association for Credit and Rural Assistance).

EMBRAPA: Empreza Brasileira de Pesquisa Agropecuária (Brazilian Agriculture and Cattle Research Agency).

FUNRURAL: Fundo de Assistência e Previdência de Trabalhador Rural (Foundation for the Aid and Welfare of Rural Workers).

IBAMA: Instituto Brasilero do Meio Ambiente (Brazilian Environmental Institute), a new environmental protection agency.

INCRA: Instituto Nacional de Colonização e Reforma Agraria (National Institute for Colonization and Agrarian Reform). Carried out the colonization scheme.

INPA: Instituto Nacional de Pesquisas da Amazonia (National Research Institute of the Amazon) in Manaus.

MA: Ministerio de Agricultura (Ministry of Agriculture).

MIRAD: Agency that took over some frontier administrative responsibilities (land titles) from INCRA.

PACAL: Projeto Agroindustrial Canavieira Abraham Lincoln (Agroindustrial Cane Project Abraham Lincoln—Km. 92 of Altamira-Itaituba highway).

PIN: Programa de Integração Nacional (Program for National Integration). Created INCRA and Transamazonian colonization.

SUCAM: Superintendência de Contrôle da Malária (Superintendency for Malaria Control).

SUDAM: Superintendência de Desenvolvimento da Amazonia (Superintendency of Amazonian Development).

ACKNOWLEDGMENTS

This has been a three-year project, so I have many people to thank. Thanks go first to my parents and grandparents, who inspired me to ramble out into the world and be curious; to my brothers, who thrashed me regularly as a child to make me tough enough to withstand difficulties, they said; and especially to my mom, who gave not only emotional but also financial support for my undergraduate venture. Special thanks to Bill Byrne and Kate Clark, both of whom read this as a thesis, then put their artistry to work revising the figures for the manuscript. To my roommates and friends who put up with three years of readings, re-readings, and my jabbering about subjects in which they were not necessarily interested—Dave, Eric, Riaz, Kathy, Kristina, Tôn—my ever-lovin' gratitude. And to Jeff, wherever he may be.

The research was made possible by two grants, one from Undergraduate Research Opportunities and one from the Center for Latin American Studies at Stanford. Special thanks go to Dr. William and Sally Massy, who donated the money for the Undergraduate Research Opportunities Golden Grant, and to all those donors whose names I don't know. A Humanities Center Grant for the Arts allowed me to spend time turning parts of this thesis into a story. All the people who have administered these grants and put up with proposals and problems—Laura Selznick at URO, Sharon, Nora, Kathleen, and wonderful Jutta at Bolivar, and Shirley Bryce-Heath and Linda at Humanities Center—you are all amazing. The Museu Paraense Emilio Goeldi provided an academic home-away-from-home and the link to great people and researchers—Luis, Denny, Sydney, and the linguistics gang. Ricardo and Luciana Nassif helped make that connection.

My thanks to all those who have given informal advice, corrections, and expertise en route—Dr. Eytan Bercovitch, Dr. Bill Durham, Dr. Terry Karl, Glenn Switkes, and Dr. Susanna Hecht. Special accolades to Karin

Van den Dool, who earned Teacher of the Year in my book for making my Portuguese passable in five short months.

I would especially like to thank my two primary advisors, Professors Emilio Moran and Stephen Haber. Emilio Moran's help in Belém gave this study shape and substance—in his class on Ecological Anthropology in the Tropics at the Museu Goeldi and over long dinners when he provided the critical background information on his two decades of research as well as access to questionnaires and field notes. After my return he read more than one draft of chapters during the thesis stage and gave it technical polish in places it was lacking. Steve Haber has seen this project from beginning to end, from when questions were "Which do you think, Brazil or Chile?" to when they became "ANOVA or t-test?" An undergrad couldn't ask for a better advisor.

In turning this from thesis to book, again I thank Emilio Moran, who sent it to the right people at the right press, right off the bat. Dr. Nigel Smith provided a most helpful and detailed critique as I readied the manuscript for publication, and later sent articles and more advice. Doug Clark, Stephanie Choi, and Kristina Pappas helped with a final reading, while Julie Turetsky, a fellow teacher at Jordan Middle School, added an English teacher's touch. I would also like to thank my 6th graders for putting up with a bleary-eyed teacher while I revised the manuscript for publication. Palo Alto Unified School District provided both support and equipment, especially for the creation of some of the figures. The people at the University of Texas Press calmed all fears and answered all questions.

Finally, I would like to thank the "informants" whom I cannot name but have given pseudonyms that I hope they would find fitting or at least amusing—the Side Road 27 community, the Mayor of '68, CIRA-PACAL members, Rapaz, Sandman, and all those who transported, fed, and housed me. The Bemvindos were like a second family, and I cannot thank them enough. I only hope these people's hospitality, generosity, and strength of character come through in this writing.

I will present the information I gathered, then argue my interpretations. Often I quote informants and borrow from their conclusions, mostly because I believe they are the experts on their situation. Ultimately, the conclusions are my own.

PREFACE

After the trees in Amazonia,
a colonist farmer walks among
charred trunks, planting seeds in the
ash. Legumes spread their tendrils,
manioc branches reach for the sky,
birds dip down to lunch on seeds and
leave their droppings. The droppings
contain seeds for a new forest, a
colonizing forest. A rainforest died
and life blooms. But what quality of
life? What complexity of life? Were
some life-forms forever lost in the
burn? After the trees, we wonder.

I wrote this as an undergraduate thesis. Simple curiosity brought me to the Amazon. Concern over deforestation inspired my study. The thesis project took two and a half years, start to finish. In the two years after its completion, I graduated twice, once with a BA in history and Latin American Studies and once with a master's in education. The second degree landed me a job at Jordan Middle School in Palo Alto, California.

As of the final revision, spring 1993, I teach sixth graders. Sixth graders are God's gift: curious, mostly civilized, and somewhat informed. They're not the most abstract of thinkers, but they see many lights that the enlightened might overlook. They like to see the big picture, and they want it simple. Somehow I wanted to make all of this relevant for them. A teacher who can't answer the question "Who cares?" shouldn't be teaching the material. So I tried to think of how Amazonian colonization and deforestation fit into the big picture.

I presented it in terms of progress: what we call progress often carries a cost. In the case of the Amazon, we measure the cost in lost forest species. I told my students about farmers I'd met who had once scraped by as landless workers but who now own small farms and raise healthy families. In order to prosper, they cleared and burned their land. Any number of bird, insect, reptile, fungus, and fish species may have perished from the torch or from later herbicides, pesticides, fungicides, and erosion. What species? How many? Nobody knows. We mourn their extinction. Will we deliver ourselves the same fate? We can only speculate how the losses of species and ecosystems will affect the human species in the long run. As we mark more and more ecosystems for extinction, we threaten the global niche into which we evolved over millions of years. How long do we want to sustain ourselves, and what kind of life do we want to sustain? That is a question I put to my students.

After I gave them a two-day slide show on deforestation in the Amazon, my sixth graders decided they needed to do something about "this global warming thing." One suggested, "If everybody on earth planted one tree a week, we'd have billions and trillions of new trees." True, said I, but how do we convince five billion people to plant trees? And who would provide the seedlings? Change begins within, with one person and one seedling. Together, we pared down our goals to growing a garden and building a greenhouse on our own campus. We will explore the garden across the curriculum, studying native, drought-resistant plants of California. Eventually, we'd like it to become a nursery of native plants, to provide seedlings for the community. Some day, maybe European grasses will become a rarity in California, as native grasses retake our hillsides, our backyards, our playgrounds.

Considering my undergraduate passion and expertise, one might expect that I'd take up a collection at school to save the rainforest, to buy ourselves some prime acreage in the tropics. I'm not a big fan of students buying acreage of rainforest. What the schoolchildren would really have to buy in Brazil is gunmen to keep squatters and land barons off the land. Kids hiring gunmen never appealed much to me. My work suggests students would be better off raising money to buy forest products. Such purchases provide forest peoples and their tropical nations the opportunity to earn a living from their precious natural resources. Spices, fruits, lumber, medicinal plants, and other forest products make use of the biodiversity that we consider so valuable in the abstract.

Brazilians rightfully see Americans as meddlers; we're quick to point out global problems, but tortoise-slow to fix or even admit our own. As you read the story of colonization and deforestation on the Transamazon Highway in these pages, consider that Amazonia mirrors the history of our Western frontier. Americans have little right to dictate policies across hemispheres as we clear-cut the nearest National Forest and drain the nearest marsh. We who observe and comment on other lands have a responsibility to heal our own.

1

AMAZONIA: WHY COWS?

*After the trees in Amazonia,
heavy black smoke belches up through
a gap in the canopy created by the
Caterpillar D-8. Ahead and beside
the blade lies forest rubble, clods of
purple earth still sticking to exposed
roots. Behind, the unbroken track of
barren soils leads back to the
highway. A new road crawls into the
forest. A turtle limps away and down
a bulldozed streambed, bathing in
the red murk of erosion beyond. In
years to come, the swath of road cut
by the tractor will widen and splinter
into the forest as* colonos *and*
glebistas *carve their farms
into the landscape.*

When military President Emílio
Garastazú Médici proposed construction of the Transamazon Highway in
1970, the Brazilian media depicted a road stretching out through a flat expanse of mature forests, its surface paved with glittering stones and precious metals—purported riches of the Amazon yet to be discovered. The
highway held a promise: Brazil of the future. Planners drew lines on maps
which reflected their utopian vision. They paid little heed to the soils, the
swamps, or the hills over which the highway would be laid. From a plane,
the Amazon basin looks like a level and unending stretch of green, broken

The highway: a woman and her son catch a ride to
town along the Transamazon Highway.

only by the serpentine paths of rivers. The whole expanse appears peaceful, plentiful, and easy to cross with a highway. But the forest deceives.

The trip from Belém to Altamira taught me much about the region and its highway, the Transamazon (Fig. 1.1). It took three days to traverse the one thousand kilometers—three days, six buses, three boats, and a ten-hour hitch with a truck driver named Eduardo. The trip back to Belém took an hour by plane. Through rain and mud the vehicles swerved to avoid ditches where the highway had been washed away because of lack of drainage. One night our bus stopped to let passengers walk across a half-fallen bridge. Beams, one foot wide by thirty feet long, were missing where the tires of the bus would normally pass. The beams had been washed out during the rainy season, and the government had yet to replace them. The heavy equipment used to fix bridges was hard to move during the rainy season, and the government was generally slow in responding to problems, Eduardo told me. They would be lucky if the bridge were rebuilt by mid-summer, but it would probably be washed out again during next year's rains. Drivers slowed to twenty kilometers an hour, then fifteen in order to creep up a steep grade, bogging down in holes two feet deep that had looked like harmless mud puddles. When going downhill, they made up time with a vengeance. On big potholes the bus or truck went airborne. What had happened to the planners' utopian vision?

The plans for the highway had called for pavement. The government told international creditors and prospective colonists that it would be paved. It was never paved. So when Eduardo and I stopped at a family run store for beers and a chat, I asked Eduardo why they didn't pave it.

Não têm condições, he said, "Because they don't have the means." They do not have the cash, the tractors, the cement, or the political clout in Brasília. The answer became a rallying cry I heard daily during my fieldwork. Why is there no medicine at the health post? Why can't they hire a teacher? Why can't anyone get a loan from the bank? *Não têm condições*. This book is about Amazonian colonists finding the *condições*, the means to survive and prosper on the frontier today.

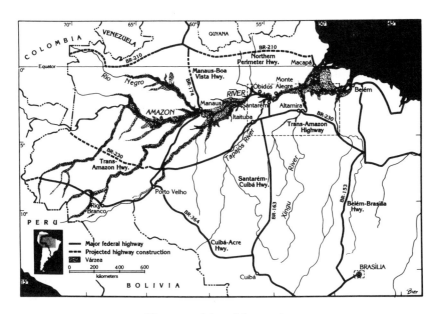

Figure 1.1: Map of Amazonia.
(From Stephen Bunker, *Underdeveloping the Amazon* [Urbana: University of Illinois Press]. © 1985 by the Board of Trustees of the University of Illinois.)

Development from the Top Down

Brazilian governments have always looked at the Amazon as a source of untapped wealth. The plethora of life it supported in mature rainforests promised untold riches when converted to modern agricultural and mineral production. Until 1964, the Amazon remained largely under mature forests.[1] A military government seized power in a coup that year. International banks and multinational corporations provided massive loans and technical assistance to support the new government's agenda to modernize the country. Brazil began "developing" the Amazon.

The central government expropriated millions of hectares of Amazonian lands for redistribution. In 1970, the government commenced construction of the Transamazon Highway to open Amazonia for exploitation and colonization. The Amazon's promise of riches would soon be tested. Colonists and cattle ranchers poured in, laying claim to the so-called virgin lands. They wrote their claims with chain saws, fire, fences, and blades of grass.

Development policies led to massive deforestation. By 1988, Brazilians had deforested 8–10 percent of the Amazon by conservative estimates.[2] Estimates based on Landsat photographs placed the figure nearer to 12 percent.[3] Such figures may seem low to the catastrophists and low in comparison to those for countries like Costa Rica, Madagascar, or the Ivory Coast. But 12 percent of the Brazilian Amazon equals 600,000 square kilometers—roughly one and a half Californias. Due to the rainforests' incredible biodiversity, every square kilometer deforested can mean extinction for untold species of plants and animals.

In 1975, Robert Goodland presented a nightmare scenario in his book *Amazon Jungle: Green Hell to Red Desert?*, predicting deforestation would transform much of Amazonia into desert. He warned that misguided development policies of the early 1970s were promoting deforestation on a scale that could turn the Amazon's lateritic soils into one great red brick. Goodland was only partially correct in his prophecy. Laterite does harden with prolonged exposure to rain and sun; but lateritic (now known as plinthitic) soils actually cover less than 5 percent of the Amazon basin, so that, contrary to his predictions, vegetation does recover in most of the deforested areas. This says nothing of the quality of vegetation, however. Today the traveler finds a different but perhaps equally destructive scenario. In the wake of chain saws and fire and the ever-expanding network of roads, cattle ranches spread across the frontier, turning verdant forests into pasture and

Pasture and stumps: pasture grass and charred stumps cover this lot of infertile white sand soils. Mature upland forest lines the distant ridge.

degraded scrubland. Driving along the Transamazon Highway, one sees primary forests only from a great distance. Pastures, weeds, and secondary forests stretch out on both sides of the road. Vast tracts of Amazonia's forests have been converted from that "Green Hell" to an Amazonian version of Green Acres.

Ecologically and economically, cattle ranching seems to be the worst possible land use in Amazonia.[4] In mature forests, people can collect forest products ranging from lumber, vines, and other building materials to fruits, nuts, meat, and medicines. In mature pasture, people collect mostly cows. We should not knock cows—they provide manure, milk, cheese, meat, and leather for a farm family. They even contribute to the greenhouse effect with their methane emissions. One could argue that ruminants are the wave of the future in natural grasslands. But one could hardly argue that cows provide as diverse a harvest as the forest. Indigenous and forest peoples, with their complex understanding of the forest, have learned to use forest products for subsistence while clearing only small plots for agriculture.[5] Cattle ranchers lack such an intimate understanding; they are more concerned with amassing assets than with subsisting. Consequently, Susanna

Hecht claims that 90 percent of the deforested land has been converted to pasture.[6]

Researchers have asked why this pattern of ranching emerged. Why cows? This book will attempt to answer that question.

I went to the Amazon in the summer of 1989 to examine colonist land use patterns and social development over the past twenty years. I studied the region west of Altamira on the Transamazon Highway, one of the areas first settled under the government colonization project. I asked what areas of forest colonists were cutting down, what they were planting in its place, and why.

Several researchers who arrived with colonists in the early 1970s carefully documented the Transamazon's history. They witnessed the beginnings of the current environmental crisis. Emilio Moran and Nigel Smith studied the frontier region near Altamira, Pará, during the first years of colonization and detailed human interaction with the environment.[7] Moran and Smith pointed to various pressures on the ecosystem and suggested alternative development solutions, but they could only speculate on what would become of the Transamazon.

Unfinished history left this researcher hanging. Having read all about the Transamazon of the 1970s before ever setting foot on the highway, I embarked with questions for the people I would meet: How would colonists adapt to their new environment in the long run? How would they alter the ecosystem? How would the Amazon be developed? Only time could answer these questions.

And so it has.

Over the last twenty years the frontier was subject to changes in policy, demography, the economy, and the ecosystem. Yet little research had been done since the 1970s to tell the colonists' side of the story. Here begins the tale of the Transamazon today.

Smith's and Moran's extensive research and writings enabled me to compare the frontier of twenty years ago to the frontier of 1989. I used two questionnaires based on theirs in order to obtain comparable data. I did a survey of the Altamira-Médicilandia segment of the highway for a broad perspective of the region, as Smith had done, and a community study within the region on Side Road 27, in the community where Moran did his work.[8] This combined approach provided an overview of the region as well as extended contact with one small, settled community. I present data from my fieldwork alongside a review of secondary literature to delineate some of the longitudinal changes.

Colonists' answers to my initial questions provided direction for my research. I found that the unequal distribution of land and the heterogeneity of soils have led to a preponderance (call it an excess) of cattle ranching on the frontier. Few crops except grass can grow in the majority of Amazonian soils once an area has been deforested. Farmers turn to cattle as a last resort on degraded land.

Colonists arrived at an unfamiliar ecosystem. The newcomers embarked on a program of clear-cutting and burning to convert forested areas to intensive agricultural land and pasture for cattle. Initially, they ignored the diversity of the rainforests and their soils. Over time, the poor quality of most Amazonian soils shaped the patterns of agricultural production. Today, colonists respond to the incredible diversity of the ecosystem by becoming familiar with their particular forest and plot of soil, then planting accordingly. Soils largely determine what is produced and where, so soil ecology and colonists' understanding of this aspect of their ecosystem will be discussed in detail.

Generally, colonists have adapted to the heterogeneity of their ecosystem by planting what their soils and terrain can support. Whenever possible, small holders plant the few crops that can survive on poor soils, like black pepper (*Piper nigrum*) and manioc (*Manihot esculenta*). When colonists turn to tree crops and agroforestry, the crops take on an added ecological advantage of mimicking the forest structure and protecting soils from erosion. Yet many tree crops, such as cacao and rubber, flourish only in the best Amazonian soils. I found that cattle dominate on small farms with poor soils, as those soils are unable to support most forms of intensive agriculture. Crops dominate on small farms with strong soils. Crops employ and feed more people per hectare than cattle.

However, medium and large holders plant only pasture grass and raise only cattle, regardless of soil quality. Large holders are limited by the labor demands of crops. Whereas small holders rely on family labor, large holders must hire laborers to farm their estates. Rather than planting labor-intensive crops, therefore, large holders turn to the low labor investment of cattle. Since cattle provide the lowest economic return per unit hectare deforested, large holders use the land the least efficiently from an ecological perspective. My data suggest that small holders are more likely to raise crops than cattle as compared to large holders; and farmers with rich soils are more likely to raise crops than farmers with poor soils.

In seeking solutions to the destruction by reversing current trends, this book considers possible alternatives to present policies. It examines the implications of a second land redistribution in the colonization zone, from medium and large holders to small holders and forest peoples. I will argue that a second land reform would be not only socially desirable, but also ecologically sensible and economically productive. If the Amazon is to be exploited agriculturally, small holders and forest peoples are better adapted to do so than medium or large holders.

In order to discourage large land holdings and deforestation for cattle ranching, the government might reverse its policies of the 1970s. As it once provided tax havens for those who deforested, it now might institute a progressive tax on deforested lands to make larger, deforested land holdings undesirable. Infertile areas controlled by large ranchers should be reforested. Areas not yet deforested should remain under the control of the forest peoples occupying them.

I will argue for a colonist-led redistribution through grassroots collective action, rather than a repetition of the failures of the government-directed redistribution in the 1970s. Brasília has neither the capital nor the expertise to direct frontier colonization. Colonists have developed strong communities on the frontier and have proven themselves capable of directing colonization in the absence of government controls. When faced with overwhelming obstacles—poor roads, insufficient access to health and educational services, and low prices for agricultural goods—colonists banded together in order to surmount the challenges. They built their own roads and schools, engaged in collective bargaining to improve farm prices, and in one case organized a town government to provide water and electricity when the bureaucracy (INCRA) which ran the town until 1980 provided nothing. By demonstrating their abilities to survive and prosper under frontier conditions and by banding together to achieve collective ends, colonists have proven themselves capable of directing a second land redistribution. With their specialized knowledge of the local ecosystem, colonists know best which lands should be redistributed.

Changing the land tenure system is necessarily a radical idea within the Brazilian context because it would cut to the core of Brazilian socioeconomic structure. However, such solutions seem moderate when compared with the radical inequalities of Brazil and positively rational when considered against the current economic and environmental debacle.

If my biases toward the colonists are not already evident, I admit them. It is difficult to witness a mass movement of individuals asserting their autonomy, demanding their rights, and gaining self-respect, without becoming emotionally involved. I do not believe colonists are the evil that some environmentalists think they are fighting. Colonists are caught in a dangerous position in Brazil that effectively forces them to push the "agricultural frontier" further into the forest, to continue deforestation. Unless the social, economic, and political situation changes dramatically, deforestation will continue along the destructive path it has followed thus far. This book will discuss the current pattern and suggest how colonists and land redistribution could form part of the solution to the destruction. My research points to colonists' collective action and land reform as ways of overcoming impediments that have made clear-cutting and cattle ranching the rational outcome of the prevailing political and socioeconomic conditions in the Amazon.

On the Transamazon, the forest serves as a backdrop to farms—back a kilometer or two from the road and behind the grass, the pepper stakes, the groves of manioc, and the frontier farmhouses of mud and thatch or concrete. Only once in my summer on the Transamazon did I hack into the thicket at the end of a lot to walk into the forest. The forest stands everpresent, but it stands away from and beyond the daily production of family farms. I studied the farms and the farmers, the Transamazon after the trees.

9

2

DILEMMAS OF DEVELOPMENT

After the trees in Amazonia,
the land blooms with manioc, rice,
corn, and cacao; great trucks roll out
along mud-slick roads under the
weight of an agricultural surplus.
Cattle graze on colonião grasses
brought from Africa, the continental
cradle of humankind.

When Brazil's military government conceived the Transamazon development scheme, a centralized bureaucracy formulated and executed policy, imposing development from the top down. Initially, the land expropriated was slated to be redistributed to small family farmers who had been pushed out of the more developed regions of Brazil. Eventually, colonist small farmers would be pushed aside in the Amazon as well.

The military government set conflicting goals for its frontier policy. On the one hand, the military wanted to appease populist forces in the country, who demanded equitable distribution of wealth. On the other hand, it followed economic growth policies which concentrated wealth in the hands of the few—so that the pie would eventually grow for all. The latter policy has come to be known as the "Trickle Down" theory in the United States. To satisfy the populists, the government expropriated a 200-kilometer-wide swath of land across 3,000 kilometers of the Amazon basin. It slated this land for redistribution to poor and landless family farmers. As growth slowed throughout Brazil, the military government reneged on its first goal of redistributing land to the poor and returned to its second goal of Trickle Down economic growth by redistributing Amazonian land to the wealthy.

In order to comprehend the situation colonists currently face, one must understand Transamazonian history. This chapter provides a background on the Transamazonian development scheme, along with reasons given by the military government for the scheme and the ideologies driving Brazilian progress and development today.

Historical Overview of the Transamazon Development Scheme

Prior to 1964, Brazilian development concentrated almost exclusively in the Northeast and the South. Both regions offered fertile soils that were accessible to ports on the Atlantic for shipping products to market—primarily to Europe and North America. Brazil followed a single crop export model for much of its history. In the sixteenth and seventeenth centuries, a sugar boom, then bust, triggered development and decline in the Northeast; in the nineteenth and early twentieth centuries, a coffee bonanza shifted economic power to the South as the Northeast declined. The Northeast never recovered. Through most of this period, the Amazon served Brazil as a frontier of extraction for export to Europe and America, providing raw materials such as Brazil wood, Brazil nuts, rubber, quinine, and cacao.

In the latter half of this century, Brazil's development strategy changed. From a primary product exporter with a heavy dependence on coffee, Brazil became the tenth largest industrial power in the world. The industrial sector expanded from cotton textiles to heavy machinery and automobiles. Agriculture expanded and diversified as well.

Production on many of the best lands in the South and Northeast shifted from small scale or subsistence farming to export-oriented, capital-intensive agriculture on large land holdings. After the price of soybeans doubled on the world market in 1973, corporate farmers converted lands with fertile soils in the state of São Paulo from red bean production for Brazilian consumption to soybean production for export. Ironically, Brazil must now import the staple red beans to make up for lost production while depending on continued strength in world markets for its export crops.[1]

Agricultural exporters earned some of the foreign capital so crucial to financing industrial expansion. Multinational corporations and international banks provided much of the rest. Between 1964 and 1980, Brazilian economic growth fluctuated between 8 percent to 12 percent. Economists dubbed this industrial transformation the "Brazilian Miracle" and hailed it as a model for other developing nations. Developments in the Amazon were an extension of this rapid growth.

The poor and the Amazon became, in the words of Shelton Davis, "victims of the miracle."[2] Growth in agricultural output was driven, not by increasing efficiency or the Green Revolution, but by clearing new lands.[3] Small and tenant farmers were pushed or bought off their prime lands by agribusiness. These farmers faced a choice: either become wage laborers, with hopes for a high paying job in the ever-expanding industrial sector, or buy land elsewhere. Many found nothing. The notorious *favelas* (slums on the hills of Rio de Janeiro) and the growing slums of São Paulo testify to their numbers. Some remained in the countryside to become *sem terras*, landless rural workers. Those who had the means to buy new farms placed demands on the government to make land more available and more affordable for the small farmer. The government did nothing. Shut out from lands in Brazil's central areas of production, landless Brazilians began spontaneous occupation and colonization of the Amazonian frontier.[4]

Then in 1970, a third year of severe drought in the chronically underdeveloped Northeast caused widespread hunger and social unrest.[5] Meanwhile, the population grew at a rate of 3 percent a year, increasing the number of mouths to feed and the demands for affordable land. The military government answered those demands in 1970 with land reform, not in the Northeast or South, but on the economic and cultural periphery—in Amazonia. The government began constructing the Transamazon Highway to open the Amazon for exploitation and colonization.

The land reform and colonization program, entitled Programa por Integração Nacional (Program for National Integration) or PIN, called for the construction of 14,000 kilometers of highway throughout the Amazon to be colonized by family farmers. The government expropriated a zone 100 kilometers wide along both sides of the highway for redistribution, totaling over 2.2 million square kilometers.[6] Much of the area expropriated had been occupied by indigenous peoples and Amazonian peasants in the first place. Most of the land was eventually redistributed as *glebas* (farms greater than 500 hectares) for use by large landholders, as discussed below. The redistribution was hardly a move toward social justice.

The government organized INCRA (the National Institute for Colonization and Agrarian Reform) to carry out the PIN program. Side roads would branch off the highway every five kilometers to make these lands accessible. Roads opened the Amazon for the exploitation of lumber, mineral, hydrological, and agricultural resources, which Brazil has exploited with a vengeance.[7] The Grande Carajás iron ore mining project alone produces U.S.$450 million annually, but attendant environmental and social costs have been quite high. Road building also made vast tracts of forest, then occupied by subsistence and extractive forest peoples, accessible to colonists and cattle ranchers. Thus, according to sociologist Stephen Bunker, "The Amazon passed from being an extractive periphery of Northern European and North American economies to being the peripheral frontier for the Brazilian economy."[8]

On the highways and side roads, the government planned to settle 100,000 families, primarily from the troubled Northeast. Each family would receive a 100-hectare lot or one square kilometer. Through a program termed *urbanismo-rural* (rural urbanism), INCRA offered prospective colonists the advantages of urban living in an agricultural environment. While working on their own lots, colonists would live in government-built towns called *agrovilas*, complete with schools and health posts along with forty-eight identical houses. At least that was the plan.

By 1978, INCRA had settled only 7,674 households.[9] *Agrovilas* also met their demise. Most colonists preferred living on their own lots to commuting on foot from the *agrovilas*. The government-built houses were abandoned, moved piece by piece to lots, or occupied by wage laboring families.

Government support for the Transamazon scheme changed as well. Due largely to forces outside the government's control, Brazil entered an economic stagnation after the oil crisis of 1973 and outright decline after renewed price increases in 1980. However, Brazil's generals should take some blame for their centralized mismanagement. With a burgeoning foreign debt, financial resources which had been so abundant soon went to the worsening deficit. Whereas the government had encouraged cultivation of staple crops (corn, rice, and beans) for internal consumption prior to 1973, afterward it encouraged export crops, such as sugarcane, coffee, black pepper, and cacao, which could earn greatly needed foreign exchange.[10] The government also favored "key sectors"—mining, livestock, lumber, large scale agriculture, and tourism—that policymakers believed had high potential either to generate foreign exchange through exports or to conserve it through the substitution of imports.[11]

Between 1973 and 1980, the government devoted fewer and fewer resources to the colonization project—failing to provide some of the education and health support promised to colonists in 1970. By 1980, INCRA was virtually disbanded in the state of Pará. While it once dealt with education, welfare, community activities, and road building, INCRA now simply signs over titles on its millions of hectares of untitled land. The government failed to uphold its promises. After 1980, colonists were left to fend for themselves. Colonists responded to the vacuum that resulted from this abrupt end to government services by engaging in collective action. When the government failed, the colonists began to provide roads, education, and health services for themselves.

The military government's path of economic development might be termed "socialism for the rich." Government-funded development programs like the Transamazon scheme funneled state resources into the hands of an elite few. The military government hired Brazilian conglomerates, in conjunction with multinationals, to build roads, dams, and nuclear power plants. Roads provided access to state resources such as minerals and timber; power plants provided low cost electricity to growing industries. Thus the wealthy became the primary beneficiaries of those roads and power plants. By directing income upward, the government helped individuals amass capital, hoping the individuals would reinvest the capital in industrial growth—not unlike the Reagan-Bush era in the United States.

The government paid for such programs by borrowing foreign capital. These policies spurred one of the greatest periods of sustained economic growth in Brazilian history. When the rapid growth ended, social inequality remained, as did the government's enormous debt, much of it owed to foreigners—again, not unlike the Reagan-Bush era. When the Brazilian economy worsened, the wealthy withdrew their newly amassed capital from Brazil in search of safer investment havens like Swiss banks. The government paid high returns to lure investors into the bond market. Investors who remained put their money into government bonds to finance the debt, not into job-creating industries. Productivity stalled as inflation soared. Government workers continued to demand pay increases adjusted to inflation. The debt crisis ensued, and the miraculous growth ground to a halt. In the end, the autocrats quietly relinquished power, leaving the democrats to clean up the mess.

Government debt and capital flight continue to hamper Brazil's economic growth. The International Monetary Fund, the West's creditor of last resort for debt-ridden governments, pointed to protectionism and big government populism as the cause of the downfall of an otherwise enlightened capitalist regime. In Brazil as elsewhere, the IMF prescribed "austerity" measures as a panacea for the debt crisis. Governments from Poland to Argentina cut salaries, staffs, and social programs to satisfy IMF requirements and maintain international credit ratings. In 1993, as we in the United States find ourselves in something of a debt crisis, we debate whether or not to raise taxes on gasoline by seven cents a gallon and how much we should trim from a $30 billion space station. Understandably, those who suffered austerity in the 1980s at the hands of the U.S. financed International Monetary Fund resent the bitter medicines we willingly prescribe for others but not for ourselves.

Objectives of PIN

The original PIN plan served three objectives for the military regime: social, military, and economic. Two were spelled out in slogans used to promote the scheme. The first advertised *Terra sem homens para homens sem terra*, "Land without men for men without land."[12] INCRA did provide land for the landless, although not on the scale envisioned by the original plan. The government hoped to alleviate social pressures while gaining popular support. With the land reform and cooperative programs set up by INCRA (discussed in chap. 6), the authoritarian regime made a populist appeal for political legitimacy. Many saw the slogan as deceptive. Amazonia already had men—and women and children too—but most of those were indigenous peoples and *caboclos* (a somewhat pejorative term used to describe backwoods people), as peripheral to Brazil culturally and economically as the Amazon was geographically. These forest peoples were a mix of colonists from the early 1950s, rubber tappers from the turn of the century, "acculturated" descendants of indigenous peoples, and some "unacculturated" indigenous peoples (notably the Arara, Kararaô, and Assurini in the Altamira region). In other words, this stretch of forest was well-occupied before the highway was built. Some of these forest peoples became successful colonists. Many were pushed out or aside. The military generals' National Integration slogan/war cry to bring "men without land to a *land without men*" was painfully mistaken. To be more accurate, the slogan might have read, "land without *an influential landed élite* for men without land."

The second slogan appealed to nationalism: *Integrar para não entregar*, "Integrate Amazonia so as not to lose it."[13] The military, ever concerned with sovereignty and national security, had always been uneasy with Brazil's extensive and undefended borderlands occupied by people with few ties or allegiances to the national metropole.[14] PIN's highways would facilitate defense against purportedly hostile forces from without (land hungry bordering nations) and control over an independent population within.[15] When colonized by people from the Northeast and South, Amazonia would gain cultural and economic ties to the rest of the country.

The third objective, not given a slogan, was economic. Brazil wanted to exploit its own natural resources. Though downplayed in the original PIN plan, economics became an overriding factor in later Amazonian "development." When faced with an economic crisis in 1973, the government reverted to its old formula of growth without equity. It shifted policy in Amazonia away from nominally supporting small homesteaders to promoting the sale of *glebas*—large areas of rainforest set aside for corporate farming. Those who came to own huge tracts of land became known as *glebistas*. In the government's own words, "At first, we were concerned with settling farmers on their land. Today, the situation is different and we feel that large companies, exploiting extensive areas, are called for."[16] Apparently the government did not intend to carry out the "for men without land" part of the old slogan either. The colonization program, initiated in the name of social justice, actually perpetuated the pattern of radically unequal land distribution found in the rest of Brazil (and Latin America).

The shift in land distribution policy led to the famed tax credit subsidies for giant cattle ranches. In order to avoid taxes, corporations and wealthy individuals simply cleared rainforests. Whether they produced anything apparently made little difference in the eyes of the government. Corporate ranchers used cattle as nothing more than a smoke screen for land speculation.[17] Hecht and Cockburn summarize the results:

> In a state like Pará, almost 90 percent of the holdings were on less than 240 acres [100 hectares], the standard colonization lot, and occupied 20 percent of the area in private hands. They employed 82 percent of the rural labor force and produced more than 65 percent of the aggregate value in agriculture. Holdings greater than 2,400 acres [1,000 hectares] gobbled up about 60 percent of the area in private hands, absorbed about 3 percent of the labor and produced only 13 percent of the value in agriculture.[18]

Favoring large holders had serious implications for the economy as well as the environment. As Hecht and Cockburn state, small holders employ far more people and achieve a higher agricultural output per unit of deforested area than large holders. If the government intended to raise economic output by relying on corporate farming, it blundered.

Perspectives on Progress and Development

The banner on the Brazilian flag reads *Ordem e Progresso* ("Order and Progress"). During the Transamazon's development, the military had something of a monopoly on order; but Brazilians have wrestled with the theme of progress throughout their history. With contending world views, a Brazilian army general, an Amazonian colonist, an Amazonian Native American, and an American researcher will often hold radically different assumptions. These assumptions should be explored briefly in order to understand the pressures behind colonization, deforestation, and preservation.

As a disclaimer, material written on the subject of Brazilian history and development since the 1960s has tended toward polemics. The successive military regimes from 1964 to 1985 in Brazil stood as a bulwark against communism and a model for economic growth. Brazil's defenders held up the country's economic growth as a model for emerging industrial nations; Brazil's detractors pointed to the slums, the pollution, and the repression that emerged during the military regime. Those who sang praise for economic growth saved their ire for the communist hordes; those who criticized military policies sometimes made veiled references to a coming revolution. Literature on Brazil typifies Cold War mentalities and Cold War blinders. The year I went to the Amazon, the Berlin Wall fell. The blinders should follow suit. In our post–Cold War world, we search for a way to interpret a history skewed by bipolar ideologies.

Military Government

The PIN scheme outlined above speaks volumes on the military regime's perspective of progress. The military government that directed Transamazonian development followed a simple formula: growth in the Gross National Product equals development. According to classic development economics, such GNP growth requires capital accumulation in the hands of capitalists who, by the nature of their class, reinvest the capital to stimulate more growth and more capital accumulation. This leads to inequity during the initial stages of capital accumulation, but eventually rapid growth increases the size of the GNP pie. Those whose standard of living fell in the initial stages should benefit from growth in the long run.[19] The military can claim some success for the period between 1964 and 1980 when measured on its own terms.

Colonists

Whereas the government initiated and directed Amazonian colonization and development through the 1970s, during the 1980s the government pulled out. Colonists now do the directing. Theirs might be considered a pre-industrial approach to development, hearkening back to that of John Locke: "As much land as a man tills, plants, improves, cultivates, and can use the product of, so much is his property."[20] Farmers on the Transamazon even use Locke's terminology, calling deforested areas *beneficiado* — "improved." By clearing and tilling the land, farmers increase production. In ecological terms, their labor redirects the energy of the ecosystem toward human consumption.

Colonists are not so keen as the military on radical disparities in wealth distribution. Frontier farmers do not believe the process of development necessitates winners (those with capital) and losers (the rest). They believe that those who improve the land, not some urban industrialist, ought to enjoy the fruits of their labor. More labor, more production, more progress: this is development.

Such reasoning justifies the clause in the new Brazilian Constitution entitling "improved" land to the person who improved it.[21] Brazilians deforest untitled lands in order to gain title to them. "Improved" lands are not subject to expropriation. Roads opened millions of hectares of untitled, mature forest lands to colonists and cattle ranchers. Cattle ranchers have built fortunes by hiring crews to deforest untitled land and staking their claim under Brazilian law, while evicting former occupants, the forest peoples. The Brazilian Constitution sanctions this injustice. Between 1985 and 1989, during the transition from a military to a civilian government, landed interests feared that their tenuous claims to forested lands would not be honored if an incoming democratic regime did not favor business interests so highly. The new government might give back the land that large holders had recently taken from small holders, squatters, and indigenous peoples. Consequently, "the threat of expropriation triggered a spasm of deforestation among property owners, since it was harder to expropriate lands if they were in some notional form of use."[22] The devastation that followed is well chronicled and peaked in 1987.

"Improvement" or deforestation by colonists is integral to the history of our hemisphere. The Brazilians are doing what Western peoples have always done: colonizing marginal lands to push out the agricultural frontier. In 1607, North America was one big hardwood forest from the Eastern Seaboard to the Mississippi. Within 300 years, little of that forest remained. Now much of that land is cultivated. Though the issue of global warming has gained a high profile in the last ten years, New Englanders recognized changes in local temperature and hydrology due to deforestation as early as the 1790s.[23] Our generation of Americans shares in these "improvements." Like North American pioneers, Brazilian colonists and governments have long viewed deforestation as a step toward progress.

Forest Peoples

The people from whom the land was taken hold their own views on progress. Contact with the West—with the disease, impoverishment, and slavery that ensued—decimated the indigenous peoples of the Americas. They are increasingly confined to reservations, on a fraction of the land they once occupied. For example, Ailton Krenak, leader of the Union of Indigenous Nations of Brazil (a political union of some 300 tribes), is one of the few remaining Krenak Indians. His people have been reduced from more than 2,000 Indians in 1920 to about 150 today. They, as a result of invasion by ranchers, live on less than a tenth of the land they formerly occupied.[24] For Krenak's people, Western development of the Amazon thus far could hardly be considered progress.

European colonizers often considered indigenous peoples to be "primitive hordes" who stood in the way of "progress." According to anthropologist Daryl Posey, who has worked with the Kayapó since the 1970s, nothing could be further from the truth: "The idea that native peoples hung around and were always in some stagnant state before they were contacted by white people is just not true. [Native peoples] like change, they like things that are new, they want to see what's going on."[25] Such experimental attitudes led native peoples to discover incredibly complex and productive forest management techniques that have yet to be understood by Western observers. After deforesting for agriculture, Kayapó Indians in the Xingu region continuously harvest and manage a forest throughout its succession to maturity, rather than burning new growth and replanting every year as colonists do.[26] Indigenous peoples in Brazil today make mistakes just like colonists and cattle ranchers. They are not perfect protectors of the environment, but they do appear to understand the forests better than anyone else does. As natural resources become scarce and environmental degradation reaches crisis proportions, many Westerners are discovering anew the indigenous peoples' ancient wisdom.

Native peoples believe in development, too, according to Ailton Krenak, but development that will address their needs, not necessarily the needs of the nation-state. On road projects like the Transamazon Highway he concludes:

> If that road takes into account the needs of local peoples it will be an enormous success. But if it doesn't it will be an immense disaster. We don't want to be understood as being against development. I would never feel happy to say that the road should not be built. I would be quite happy, on the other hand, to sit with the government and say how one might do it in another way.[27]

Like everyone else, indigenous peoples want "developments" that will benefit them. In the region I studied, some native tribes are organizing with the colonists against large landholders to reach a compromise over who benefits from "development" and who does not.

Colonists don't necessarily see themselves in conflict with Native Americans. Colonists view the forests that they claim as empty; in relative terms, the colonists are right. The Amazon was depopulated by disease and rural-urban migration during the last 500 years. Where some estimate five million indigenous people once lived, a mere 200,000 survive today.[28] Colonists almost never meet native people face to face. The perception among colonists remains: "Look at all these empty forests and available lands." Native Americans counter that the forest is already occupied, but at lower and perhaps more sustainable population densities.

American Researcher

Who can blame the Brazilians for wanting the same opportunities we've had? Brazilians of all types can and will develop their country. The question is how. This book provides an alternative perspective on development. I studied colonist small farmers in Amazonia partly because I share an affinity with them. Much of my own perspective stems from a childhood spent on small farms in what was once a frontier.

I grew up in the Sonoma Valley, considered by people in my town to be the finest wine region in the world. (People from the Napa Valley might disagree. So might the French.) Just outside the small town of Sonoma lies a smaller town called Vineburg. Vineburg is more of a post office, really, alongside a general store. And, true to its name, Vineburg has vineyards. One vineyard is called Rhinefarm after the German land from whence its two founders migrated in the 1850s. On that same farm, the men established a family business in 1857 bearing their names, the Gundlach-Bundschu Winery. When they arrived, most of the world knew California as Gold Country. Miners bled the land of most of its gold within a generation, leaving tailings and eroded Sierra foothills for posterity. Frontier farmers sought a more sustainable venture.

I spent much of my childhood mucking around in the lake and the vineyards of Rhinefarm and some of it picking grapes and bottling wine. My friend and childhood pal, Jeffrey Towle Bundschu, is the sixth generation of Bundschus to work Rhinefarm and produce fine wines. Jacob Gundlach and Charles Bundschu left a business for their children that reaps profit and pleasure from the land, generation after generation.

The ecology of Sonoma has changed; Native Americans no longer stack clamshells fifteen feet high around the marshes of the Bay. Some birds and fish of the Bay are threatened or endangered by habitat loss. Like the gold miners', the California farmers' activities also eroded the land, drained the rivers, and destroyed wetlands. But the Bundschus live well, and their grapes grow on rolling hills and former grasslands, not the threatened wetlands. They don't use many pesticides or herbicides, usually just sulfur. A small farm like theirs couldn't compete in global soybean or wheat markets. They are specialty crop farmers. They grow, process, and package their grapes right on the farm, turning truckloads of grapes worth $750 a ton into wine sold at $75 a gallon. Some agricultural ventures are more sustainable and profitable than others.

Brazilians migrate to the Amazon from the Northeast and South to find opportunity, just as my ancestors migrated to California from Ireland, Scotland, and the East Coast four, five, and six generations ago. Brazilian colonists turn to specialty crops for which they have an ecological advantage. Brazil stands poised for economic growth, once Brazilians put their political house in order.

Preservation and exploitation of natural resources both speak to particular urgencies. Those who call for growth and exploitation of natural resources call for higher standards of living so that the poorest can feed themselves and their children. Those who call for a clean, safe, beautiful, and diverse environment want the same improvements and believe they can be achieved—but only if we avoid denuding the earth. All speak of "managing" resources, "managing" the planet. Some balances must be struck. The Amazon may offer a model for the rest of the world in finding a balance.

Lessons from Amazonia

At the outset of Transamazonian colonization, the government made an attempt to reconcile environmental concerns with economic growth and social justice. Modern agricultural practices, claimed environmentalists, would destroy the ecosystem. They feared the forests would be decimated as the forest peoples had been over the last five centuries. In order to palliate the environmentalists' demands, the government dictated that colonists could deforest only half of any parcel they held, while the other half must be maintained as reserve.[29] This law was never vigorously enforced and was generally ignored by those farmers with the means to deforest greater areas. But the preservation law set the stage for one of the longest and largest scientific experiments ever performed, headed by biologist Thomas Lovejoy of the Smithsonian Institute.

For the last twenty years, Lovejoy and his team of researchers have attempted to measure the effects of deforestation. They used the 50 percent preservation law to find forest reserves of varying sizes cut off from the surrounding forests. They have examined the long-term implications of "island ecology," when species become isolated from the rest of their ecosystem or when their feeding grounds suddenly shrink. They found that cutting away part of an ecosystem is like cutting off a human limb—the damage cripples the ecosystem. Reducing habitat size threatens not just one species, but the whole habitat. Lovejoy concluded that any shrinkage or segmentation of a rainforest ecosystem will probably result in a loss of biodiversity.[30]

Lovejoy's research in the Amazon provides lessons for the planet. His findings made him a leading spokesman for preservation of entire ecosystems rather than isolated species. U.S. Secretary of the Interior Bruce Babbit's 1993 proposal to overhaul the Endangered Species Act was inspired in part by Lovejoy's work. The endangered ecosystems proposal is intended to identify habitats that need protection before extinction crises like that of the spotted owl occur. Regardless of how loosely the Amazonian preservation policy was enforced, it shames our own forest policies. When we compare a Brazilian goal of 50 percent preservation in the colonization zone to our own quarreling over the 10 percent of old-growth redwoods remaining in the Western United States, we begin to see the hypocrisy of our demands for forest preservation at the recent Earth Summit in Rio.[31] As one U.S. delegate to the Earth Summit stated, "The United States standard of living is not up for negotiation."[32] If so, then we Americans should accept responsibility for our actions and not criticize others for similar actions. We will suffer the consequences.

Rather than attempting to impose our failed land management systems on Brazil (fencing National Parks and sacrificing National Forests in the name of development), we should encourage those within Brazil who are working toward preservation management. That means supporting colonists and forest peoples in their efforts toward more complex forest management, opening and creating markets for rainforest products here, providing preferential treatment for those products, providing technical assistance to forest peoples by funding research in advanced agroforestry techniques, and supporting research in biotechnology to find uses for rainforest species. All these options value the entire rainforest rather than the land on which it stands.

Land Ethics, Land Management, and Science

At some point, the discussion of progress and development must reach beyond economic growth and profits and delve into the realm of the aesthetic, existential, and spiritual. Geologist Richard Morris writes:

> Ancient peoples believed that time was cyclic in nature. . . . We, on the other hand, habitually think of time as something that stretches in a straight line into the past and future. . . . The linear concept of time has profound effects on Western thought. Without it, it would be difficult to conceive of the idea of progress, or speak of cosmic or biological evolution.[33]

The geological clock has proceeded through five periods of mass extinction. Each time, life regenerated to fill every niche. The number of species

Rubber tapping: EMBRAPA experiments with domesticated rubber trees. Latex flowing from the most recent cut in the bark will be collected and then weighed by agricultural researchers.

reached an all-time high as *Homo sapiens* entered the scene. We are bringing about a sixth period of mass extinction.[34]

As a species, we ought to be concerned with our own extinction. We evolved on a planet full of life. Since emerging from the trees four million years ago and standing up for a view of the African savanna, our bodies have adapted to and become dependent upon the myriad of organisms living and evolving with us. We learned to manage and manipulate our environment in order to raise our standard of living or at least to ensure survival and reproduction. We domesticated potatoes, wheat, corn, rice, livestock, and fish. Our populations boomed. Yet we wiped out whole hosts of species in the process by clearing, tilling, and planting the land, diverting rivers, and draining marshes. If we destroy the species and ecosystems with which we evolved, we may unknowingly destroy ourselves.

3

THE TRANSAMAZON TODAY

After the trees in Amazonia,
a researcher walks the quiet side
road, waving to a donkey, stopping
for butterflies.

This chapter seeks to situate colonists in a human context before embarking on a statistical analysis of the agroecosystem and deforestation. The first section of this chapter will offer some straight facts: information on background research, reasons for choosing the Altamira region and Side Road 27, and how I shaped my questionnaires. The second section tells a story: traveling on the Transamazon Highway and meeting the people who live there. The story illuminates the methodology, showing how I actually collected information in the field.

My method might be called ethnoecology, ecological anthropology, or human ecology; essentially they mean the same thing. All study human interaction with the local environment. When I found that interaction influenced by politics, economics, and frontier society, I also dealt with these issues.

Belém

Before leaving for Brazil, I had narrowed my focus to the issues of road building, colonization, and government-directed development. My research proposal drew heavily from the work of Emilio Moran. He happened to be in Brazil on a Fulbright grant that year writing a book and teaching a summer course on Amazonian human ecology at the Museu Paraense Emilio Goeldi in Belém.[1] In May 1989, a month before my scheduled departure, a Brazilian friend at Stanford gave me Professor Moran's

26

number, and I made the call. Over a scratchy connection from Brasília, a somewhat amused Moran warned me that his students would range from graduate students in biology to professors of anthropology and that he would teach the course in Portuguese. He said I'd be the only foreigner and only undergraduate in the group of twenty-five. Show up, see how it goes, he said.

With only five months of Portuguese behind me, I didn't exactly catch every nuance in the first week of class. I had had six years of Spanish, though, so Moran's Spanish accent helped. Dictionary in hand, I did serve as translator for Moran now and then when he couldn't think of a word in Portuguese. The students hailed from throughout Brazil's South and Northeast. Many had already done fieldwork, if not doctoral dissertations, in the Amazon. They taught me as much outside of class as I learned from the course material. The course surveyed works from the 1950s to current research in human ecology and the Amazon. Moran wrote the course reader; it has now been published in Portuguese and English.[2] He drew much of the material from fieldwork that he had done in the region I would soon visit and study.

Having signed up for the course, I needed a place to stay. Another friend at Stanford gave me the name of Dr. Denny Moore, an American linguist working at the Museu Goeldi. I showed up at Denny's office the day I arrived in Belém and introduced myself. That night Denny took me to a party and introduced me to all his students. One, Sidney Facundes, said he had space on the floor of his apartment and was willing to teach me the finer points of Portuguese if I would teach him English. Sidney would be my roommate for the next four weeks. Later, he gave up his own hammock and took care of me for a week when I returned from the Amazonian interior with malaria.

Sidney grew up in rural Amapá, in the northeast corner of Amazonia near Brazil's northern borders. His family had been forest people at least since the rubber boom days of the last century. By hard work and a touch of brilliance, he had earned a full scholarship to the University of Pará, then met Denny and became his trusty linguistics sidekick. Denny put Sidney's talents to work; by the age of twenty-two, Sidney had spent months at a time in the most remote parts of Amazonia studying native languages. Sidney and his friends take pride in Amazonian culture, and they showed me their city at its finest.

I arrived during the festival of *Junina*, a monthlong celebration at the end of the rainy season and the biggest party of the year. People put on traditional Amazonian outfits, dance traditional Amazonian dances, eat traditional Amazonian foods, and drink copious amounts of beer. The foods I tasted there, in Belém, opened my mind to the possibilities that lay upriver. One favorite Amazonian herb numbs the tongue; another numbs all the way down the esophagus to warm the belly. Imagine eating oyster-slime and Novocain soup. The beer washed it all down nicely. Being Irish, I felt quite at home. But I never could remember very well the names of all those foods.

Amazonian friends gave me such an introduction to their cuisine that I found myself educating the Southerners from class on the wonderful array of Amazonian foods and fruit drinks. If you ever go to Belém, try the *tapereba* shake. It's unbelievable.

My time in Belém wasn't all play. I spent four weeks there continuing with background research, working closely with Emilio Moran to refine my project and writing a seven-page questionnaire. I planned a longitudinal study covering two decades and drawing primarily from previous studies by Moran and Nigel Smith. Both studied the region just east of Altamira on the Transamazon Highway. Smith covered three such regions (around Altamira, Itaituba, and Marabá). In effect, they made many methodological choices for me—who to study, where, and what kinds of information to elicit.[3] Eventually, I chose to limit my focus to one side road (which I will call Side Road 27) east of Altamira in the area they had studied.

Moran and I discussed my project in detail. He provided pertinent journal articles, names of people I should contact in the field, and original copies of the questionnaires he and Smith had used in 1974. In addition, he showed me copies of Maryanne Schmink's and Phillip Fearnside's old questionnaires. When writing my own, I used all these materials. Luis Donisete Benzi Grupione, a friend from Moran's course, helped put the finishing touches on my questionnaire by smoothing out the syntax.

My questionnaire focused on how family farmers interact with their ecosystem—their farms. Many of the questions I drew directly from Moran's questionnaire so that I could use his work as a basis for comparison when I returned. I included questions on demographics, soil utilization, agricultural production, and capital equipment. The questionnaire also asked whether farmers had encountered the traditional problems of intensive agriculture in the humid tropics—crop disease, pests, weeds, soil compaction, declining fertility, and erosion. If so, I wanted to know what steps farmers were taking to overcome these. I predicted that colonists would increasingly come to understand the heterogeneity of their ecological setting over time and adapt accordingly to utilize its potential. The interesting questions would be how the colonists adapted, how they had changed the landscape, and why.

In addition to using the questionnaires, I brought a statement to read before interviews, required by the Stanford Human Research Subjects Committee, which guaranteed complete confidentiality and requested consent. All informants gave consent before I did interviews. Most thought me strange for asking. When possible, I asked before taking photographs.

To protect confidentiality, all names of informants have been changed here, along with names for the locations of Side Road 27 and Vila Roxa. Union and cooperative presidents and government officials gave consent to quote them, but I do not provide their names either. Since completing my field research, at least two union leaders in the state of Pará have been shot and killed as a result of their political activism over land tenure and colonist and Indian rights. (I could not discern from the *New York Times* articles I have read whether they were men I interviewed.) Some people understandably prefer to be off-the-record on certain controversial statements of opinion.

While in Belém, my Portuguese improved dramatically. By the time I reached the interior I was conversant and fluid, if not fluent. My classmates, roommates, and friends taught me the language, the culture, the dances, and the rhythms of their country. Brazil does have a rhythm of its own.

The Trip to Sandman

Boarding the bus in Belém, I felt confident that I had the necessary background information. Actually, I had little concept of what the highway would look like, of how I would be received, or with whom I would live.

I briefly revisited Smith's site near Marabá (which Smith refers to as *agrovila* Coco Chato[4]) in order to have some basis for comparison with the Altamira region. Then I arrived at Moran's primary site, an area surrounding the *agrovila* which he dubbed "Vila Roxa" in honor of its purple soils (*roxa* means purple in Portuguese).

Moran had revisited the area in 1984 and said that much had changed since his study. Most of the families he had known in the 1970s had moved. He hadn't heard much from them since 1984, especially since the deepening economic crisis. He gave me the address of a family to contact when I arrived in Vila Roxa. He thought they still lived there but wasn't sure. Nobody knew I was coming.

My destination lay beyond Altamira: a small *agrovila* of forty-eight households. It looked just like all the other *agrovilas* we had passed on the bus, with its water tower (probably out of order), health post, and two parallel streets spaced two hundred meters apart. These streets formed a U with a third street half a kilometer from the highway, with a common area in the center for the school, health post, and fields. A row of boxy little houses, each identical to the next, lined the outsides of the streets. The houses faced the common area, now overgrown by weeds and small family gardens. Long ago, all the houses had been painted white, each with the letters "MA-INCRA" stenciled above the door. Only after returning did I learn what this meant: Ministerio da Agricultura–Instituto Nacional de Colonização e Reforma Agraria (Ministry of Agriculture–National Institute for Colonization and Agrarian Reform). Most of the houses were gray from weathering, their corrugated iron roofs now red from the highway's dust. The houses had taken on their own character: here some flowers and vines creeping up the porch; there a vegetable garden in the back; a picture of a fat and sassy cow from last year's Aggie Product Distributor's calendar nailed to a door. Over the years, some houses had been painted green or yellow, but they would be gray soon enough. Foundations had settled, walls had warped, and porches drooped, creating a natural curving. The government had tried to impose bureaucratic uniformity here in the Amazon. Mother Nature won.

When doing his research fifteen years ago, Emilio Moran (remembered in this *agrovila* as Seu Emilio[5]) had lived in the second house from the highway. In the third, I was supposed to find his former next-door neighbors, Dona Flora da Souza and her husband Seu Ricardo da Souza, who had run the local store and known all the local gossip when Seu Emilio had lived there. Seu Emilio kept in touch with her and her family. She could find me a place to stay, he assured me, and she'd also be a great informant about the region's happenings. Stepping off the bus, I headed straight for the third house.

Some piglets in my path scattered with grunts of protest; chickens clucked and grudgingly moved aside. Two kids digging around in the second yard saw me marching past with my backpack and pasty-white skin.

Amazonian Gothic: a colonist couple stands in front of their *agrovila* at Vila Roxa, with MA-INCRA (*Ministerio da Agricultura — Instituto Nacional de Colonização e Reforma Agraria*) written above the door to commemorate the government bureaucracies that built the *agrovila*.

They froze, I smiled; they furrowed their brows, I waved and said, *Oi*. Not many strangers came to Vila Roxa.

Closer to the third house, I saw boarded windows and a padlock on the door. Trouble. A man tending the garden next door watched my puzzled approach with a curious enthusiasm. *Oi*, he greeted me. "Does Dona Flora live here?" I asked him. *Não, já mudou ao lote*, "She already moved to their lot." "Where?" I asked. *Travessão 27*, he said, "Side Road 27." The da Souzas lived about ten kilometers in from the highway, he explained, and Side Road 27 was four kilometers beyond this *agrovila*.

On the bus, I had seen numbered signs next to side roads: "19" . . . "20". . . . The military planners numbered the roads branching off the highway every five kilometers as Side Road 1, 2, 3, etc. They numbered villages and towns according to their distances from nearby cities on the highway. Colonists usually refer to places by numbers rather than by government given names. What colonists call "Kilometer 92" is actually

"*Agrovila* Abraham Lincoln," but everyone calls it Kilometer 92 since it is 92 kilometers from Altamira.

With the sun already directly overhead and baking away the moisture from this morning's rain, I had a long, hot walk ahead. I hiked about two of the four kilometers to the side road before catching a ride with a young couple in a fast Chevrolet. The man had a Spanish accent, so I asked where he was from. Bolivia, he told me. What was he doing here in the Amazon? He looked to the woman with a grin, then to me. Business, he said, not inviting any further questioning. The car stopped; I crawled out and thanked him for the ride, feeling a bit uneasy. The frontier highway carries more than a few dubious characters. Hence, children there are wary of strangers.

The rain had ended, and I stood on the Transamazon Highway looking down the steep, purple mudslide they call Side Road 27. I skated down, around mud puddles. The road was lined on both sides with a grass that reached above my head. Colonists later told me it was called *colonião*; it had been introduced from Africa and was now a weed. Behind the grass stood symmetrical groves of trees, their branches loaded with a yellow fruit shaped like little footballs: cacao. It grows only in fertile soils, in this *terra roxa estruturada*.[6]

Humid silence drifted through. Maybe an insect's buzz now and then, the splash when I fell into puddles, sometimes the sound of a bird wrestling the wind overhead. Mostly silence. Fifteen beautiful little butterflies of four different species vied with some flies for a pile of horse droppings on the road. The camera scared them away when it came close. Eventually they returned for the picture.

A kilometer in, the surface went from the slick, purple mud to a rockier, yellowish sand. The cacao trees disappeared, and the original forest reached high overhead, its vines dripping onto the road. A black insect that looked like a flying four-inch meat-hook whirred by my right ear, seemed to hover in front of my face as we traveled in the same direction, then edged its way left, back into the forest. This was the back part of the two-kilometer-long lots next to the highway. Due to the rockier soils and distance from the main house, the owners had left this area as forest reserve. A cacophony of birds, monkeys, insects, and rustling trees contrasted with the quiet of the cacao groves five minutes back. When I took off my broad-brimmed hat, the sounds intensified; most of the noisy creatures live in the forest's upper tangle. I walked this road every day in the weeks to come and was always delighted at this stretch where the forest remained.

32

The forest: a view of the canopy from the road that passes underneath.

Up a hill, down a hill. In another five hundred meters the road's surface became sand, white as Ipanema Beach. Where the sand began, the forest vanished. Fences and pastures took its place. Gone as well were the monstrous grasses that had lined the road where the soil was purple. Here the grass barely reached my knees. Huge pastures opened up, and the closest forest was a kilometer or more back from the road. This was not the Amazon I had imagined. It looked more like pictures I'd seen of California's Mother Lode in the 1850s—green grass blanketing rolling hills, fences lining barren roads, rickety barns dotting the landscape. Tranquillity. Every four hundred meters, driveways or paths on either side of the road led to houses and barns made of wood and mud.

At the time, this landscape made little sense to me. Now, if given a map of the geography and soils I could predict fairly accurately what portion of each farm would be used for agriculture, pasture, or forest. My new surroundings made much more sense when I left Side Road 27 five days later.

At a creek, the road split and took a strange twist. Straight ahead, a road overgrown with weeds led to the water, where huge beams were strewn— some on the sides of the creek, some in it. The wreckage indicated where a large bridge had stood. To the right, the road curved and led over a newer bridge that was small but sturdy. Beyond the creek was a square barn, more of a shack, really. In the shade of its open door sat a small, thin man in his seventies. His swollen foot was propped up on the chair in front of him. He was stripping bunches of little green balls the size of BBs from stems, dropping them into the bowl on his lap, then picking up another full stem. No hurry. Two tarpaulins near him were covered an inch thick with balls, drying in the sun. One tarp had green ones, like those in his hands. The others were gray-black and withered by sun, like the old man's skin. Black pepper. The smell of it filled the air.

He smiled as I approached. I asked if this was the way to Dona Flora's. *Sim*, he said, yes. But you must be tired. Would you like to rest, to have coffee? he asked, sounding like he had marbles in his mouth garbling his speech. After deciphering his words, I said that yes, I would, thank you. He called something I could not understand to his wife and daughter, who were washing clothes in the creek nearby. I walked through the wooden gate of the fence and unbuckled my backpack. It sagged, then dropped to the sand with a "whump." He craned his neck for a better look and asked what was in it. Everything, I said: clothes, books, toothbrush, notepads, camera, everything. His monotonous tug on the stems never faltered. I asked what had happened to his foot. A log had fallen on it fifteen days ago, he said. It would take fifteen more to heal. He had to sit while his sons worked beyond the pastures at the forest's edge, their machetes hacking away at the undergrowth to provide fuel for this summer's burn.

He introduced himself as *Senhor da Areia*—"Sandman." Not his real name, he explained, but that's what everyone called him. His entire property was covered with this white sand around us. He waved his hand toward the fields I had just passed; this was his farm. *Terra fraca*, he said, shaking his head with a grimace, "weak land."

This was my chance, I thought. I explained that I was doing research on colonist families in the area and their agriculture. I told him I had a questionnaire about his family and his crops and recited the speech required by Stanford Human Subjects Research Board:

> Participation is voluntary—you may withdraw your consent at any time, you may refuse to answer any particular questions, and you may discontinue your participation at any time. If you are not comfortable with answering any questions, please let me know. All the information you give, including your name and the name of this road, will be kept completely confidential. If you have any questions or complaints about my work let me know, or you may contact my university.

He looked perplexed, disturbed. He said, OK, but ask later. Not right now.

I became nervous, not knowing what had gone wrong and thinking, My God, what if no one here will agree to an interview? His eleven-year-old daughter walked up with a thermos full of hot coffee, easing the tension. She was small, like her father. She served me a cup, gave one to Sandman, then stood back to observe the conversation with an intent stare. Soon her mother joined us, a large woman in her mid-40s. Sandman introduced her as Dona Maria and me as Seu Douglas (pronounced Say-ew Doe-gloss). She nodded to me with a smile and said hello, then picked up a wooden hoe and started pushing the peppercorns around on the tarp, stirring the scent into the air. *Elaires?* Dona Maria called to her daughter and waited. Elaires (pronounced El-ah-ear-ease) didn't move. *Agora, Elaires!* Dona Maria prodded. Elaires snapped out of her trance. She excused herself with a shy grin and grabbed the five-gallon bucket next to the tarp.

It was four o'clock, and the sun had passed its prime: time to bring in the pepper. Dona Maria pushed the peppercorns into a pile, while Elaires scooped them up with a bucket and dumped them into a burlap sack. When the sack was filled, they had a hard time lifting it. I walked over and offered to help. They refused. I insisted, and they thought me amusing: Seu Douglas, a guest, an American, a college student, working on a farm. I had spent months in my anthropology classes discussing participant observation. Finally, here I was researching on a farm in the Amazon, participating. They were right. It was ridiculous.

We carried the two bags of green and black peppercorns, forty or fifty kilos apiece, into the barn. Along the walls inside the barn were tools, a saddle, and stacks of other burlap sacks which had rice seeping out of holes in the sides. An adobe oven with a huge metal pan on top filled about a third of the barn. This was a *casa de farinha*, where the tuber-root manioc, the traditional staple crop of Amazonia, is turned into a nutritious flour, *farinha*, through a process of grating, crushing, and cooking. I knew manioc and pepper were the only two cultivars besides grass that grew on white sand. Sandman said they planted the pepper two years before, and this was their first yield. For the thirteen years since Sandman's family moved here, manioc had most likely been the family's primary source of income and calories—manioc and cows, probably, but I didn't remember seeing many cows.

With the pepper stacked, I thanked them for the coffee and went toward my pack. Dona Maria looked surprised and said I could not go to Dona Flora's today, it was too late. I could stay here, she said. Not enough room in the house, but I could stay in the barn, said Sandman. Do you have a hammock? asked Elaires. In the backpack, I said. It was settled.

Dona Maria crossed back over the bridge to go to the house. While she prepared dinner, Elaires and Sandman gave me a taste-touch-see-smell tour of their garden. The garden surrounded what could have been a house, once, but was now two wooden and adobe walls next to a pile of adobe rubble. The palm-thatch roof had collapsed onto the heap. It had been their house.

Just before the tour I had begun writing in my note pad. I had a hard time keeping up, but recorded the following:

2/7/89 Intrevista no.1 Gleba 27, Lote 17, Trav. 27

Deusete Ferreira dos Santos. (Sandman)
Arrived at ~2:30pm—he was taking pepper off vine—log had fallen on his foot 15 days ago and will take 15 more to heal. Pepper is drying in the sun. Wife

came out to turn. Calls self Senhor da Arreia. Just helped mom and daught.
bring in pepper. 3 days (black) and one day (green) in the sun. Brought in every
night.
Soils are white sand "Terra Fraca" (see pic.'s). So he grows pimenta do reino
(black pepper), and some côco (nut), and café for family.
Lots of fruits: caju (cashew-nut on top); jabute (?) de caba[7]—shrub w/ little
fruits; manga (mangoes); jáca[8] (football sized with 1 inch pyramid spikes). Ate
yesterday. Seeds inside covered in white jelly-pulp, sweet but bland; corrante
(spiny thing the size of a golf ball looks like a Venus Fly Trap. Dries up, and
tiny seeds inside turn brilliant red when you crush them. Natural food color-
ing.); aboba (?)[9]—looks like melon w/ pumpkin vines covering ground.
Oranges.

Elaires saw that the oranges made me happy when we finally got to
them—the first fruits I'd recognized—so she picked up a bucket and collected about twenty. Time to go back to the house. We walked to the road
and over the little bridge together, through the gate and into the pasture.
Cowpies and butterflies. An old horse stood near the gate munching on
grass. His back slumped, and he had no hair left on his spine.
  The family's new house was back from the road, above a little beach on
the creek. It was different from the adobe and wooden houses on the side
road and from the wooden clones in the *agrovila*. This was simple and
small, like the others, but had walls of cement, and its corrugated roof
shined bright. Its fresh coat of paint was sky blue, with "1988" painted in
black above the door. This is our new house, Elaires said with pride. Her
brothers had built it. She said the rubble in the garden across the creek was
their old house. She had grown up there during the thirteen years her
family had lived in it. I wondered which had come first, the new house or
the collapse. Near this house was a ten-by-ten-foot shack with smoke
streaming out the top—the kitchen. There I met Elaires's seventeen-year-
old sister *Elasires* (El-ah-seer-ease) who was broad like their mother. Their
four-and-a-half-year-old sister, *Maraires* (Mar-ah-ear-ease), was playing
with her six-year-old nephew *Deniuso* (Den-ee-oo-soo), son of Sandman's
oldest daughter who lived thirty kilometers away in an *agrovila* with her
husband. With the daughters, I could never figure whose name was whose.
  Waiting for dinner outside the kitchen shack, Elaires sat with her bucket
of oranges, peeling off the outer orange skins and leaving the white covering. When only the white part was left, she cut off the top and gave the

orange to someone. We sat around sucking oranges from the holes in the top, squeezing to get the juice out of the pulp, then sucking again. Orange juice on tap. They peel them so the orange part does not sting the lips. They thought my way of peeling off the white part and eating the whole thing was funny . . . useless, but funny.

We were talking about the different types of fowl running around the yard (normal chickens, bald ones, spotted ones, game hens, ducks, geese, and the fat black turkey) when Sandman's two sons arrived from the fields. Each carried a machete. Both wore khaki pants tucked into rubber boots but no shirts. Though not very tall, their thickness made them seem twice the size of their shrunken father. The younger, eighteen-year-old *Alaires* (Al-eye-ear-ease), was friendly. The older, twenty-two-year-old *Ataide* (At-eye-ee-jee), was reserved, a little suspicious. They bathed in the creek, changed, and left for a nearby lot to watch Brazil play Uruguay in World Cup competition on television. This side road, twenty kilometers long, had three televisions, Elaires said.

I asked if it was common for people to go out at night. Not really, Elaires replied, just to watch soccer and to hunt. What do they hunt? I asked, my interest piqued. Pigs, mostly, she said.[10] Ever get cats? I asked. Jaguars, panthers? No, she said, they're hard to kill now. Most big cats were gone long ago, but Ataide had heard one once. I had read about hunting in the Amazon. Hunters tie hammocks in fruit trees at night and wait there with a flashlight and a gun. Nocturnal animals come to eat the fallen fruit. Big cats come to eat the animals. The hunters kill both. They especially liked the cats because the skins brought so much cash. INCRA tried to restrict hunting for skins, but the cats were hunted out of the region soon enough anyway.

The sun had set, and dinner was ready. Dona Maria brought a kerosene candle and a bowl of rice into the house. Elasires brought beans. Elaires came with eggs and fried chicken. Little Maraires brought a bowl full of *farinha* flour to pour over everything. Everything was set in front of me, the only one at the table. They all stood and watched. Won't you be eating? I asked them. We already did, they said. Sandman came to join me, and we ate with an audience.

After dinner, we all went into the living room to talk and drink coffee. Sandman and I sat facing each other at a table in the middle of the room. Dona Maria and the kids sat on couches around the table. I still had difficulty deciphering Sandman's garbled speech. At first, I thought it was my

Portuguese, but I could understand the others. Dona Maria and the daughters would repeat his words for me when I looked confused.

Having no idea how long my first questionnaire would take and knowing it was getting late, I became restless. After a few minutes the conversation started settling on the family, so I said to them, all this information is part of the questionnaire. Would now be a good time? Sandman looked very serious and puzzled. Finally he said no, outright. I didn't understand; he had said ok earlier. After an awkward silence, he said they did not have any money and could not afford it. Afford what? I asked. To take the questionnaire, he said. He thought I was charging them for the interview. In the Human Subjects speech, I thought I'd made my intentions fairly clear. I never thought to tell them it was free. Over the next few weeks, I practiced my delivery so that the participants knew exactly what I was doing.

I took down all the family's names, ages, and how many years each had had in school. Dona Maria, Elaires, and Elasires answered most of these questions. Sandman knew neither ages nor years each child had spent in school. Very few fathers did, I later discovered. What did the father do before coming? *Vaqueiro*—"cowboy," for thirty years. He was brought by a friend who worked for INCRA and given this lot because someone else had abandoned it. It had the worst soils on Side Road 27. Hence the name Sandman.

Now for the ethnoecology: Do you collect fruits or medicines from the forest? Not much; too many insects and spines. They had planted all the fruits they would want in their garden. Do you hunt in the forest? The women nodded yes, but Sandman stiffened. No, he said. Everyone looked at him, uncertain. Slowly they shook their heads, one by one. No, no one hunts. Elaires looked away. Taboo subject. He would trust me only so far. It was actually legal to hunt, even cats if the family ate them, but it had been illegal at one time. I never asked about hunting again at Sandman's house. Two days later I was invited by someone a few kilometers down the road to hunt peccaries in the forest; two weeks later I was in a canoe watching the man in front of me hunt alligators with a harpoon.

On to simpler subjects. I needed to know what crops they had planted, how many hectares of each crop, and how much they had produced. They had five hectares of rice, one of corn, less than one of beans, three of manioc, and one of black pepper. All but the manioc and pepper were for subsistence. They could plant rice and corn for a year after burning mature forest, two years if they were lucky. Then the depleted soil would support only manioc, pepper, or grass. *Terra fraca*, he said again with a frown, "weak land." He shook his head in disgust. This year an infestation of small grasshoppers called *cigarrinha* had eaten most of his rice. And birds ate most of the corn, Elasires added in desperation. He had yet to sell any pepper. The family had been surviving for the last thirteen years on subsistence levels of rice, beans, manioc, and corn, and by selling *farinha* for a small income. When birds eat the corn, the family eats less corn. His only other income could be cattle.

How much grass do you have? Thirty hectares. That must be it, I thought. Then I remembered all the grass but few cows. How many cows do you have? Five calves. Thirty hectares and five calves? With all this grass, couldn't you have more cows? *Não têm condições*, he said. Someone else used their land, putting nine cows on it. For rent Sandman kept the calves. Sandman's family had cut down much of their forest and planted all this grass, yet they had almost no cows. It takes cash to buy cows. *Não têm condições*.

After we finished the questionnaire, Sandman's twenty-three-year-old married daughter, the most forward of the bunch, shyly inquired whether they could ask me questions. Of course, I told her. What was I *really* doing here was her first question. I've always wanted to go to the Amazon was my answer. Doing a study gave me the money to get here. Then, did I have any girlfriends at home? They asked about my family and about school. Do they have forests like this where you come from? These questions I would hear again and again. In the many interviews to come, I always looked forward to this moment when they relaxed and, from honored guest and stranger, I became a person to them.

The next day, when I finally found Seu Emilio's friends, Dona Flora and Seu Ricardo da Souza, I discovered why they had moved from the *agrovila*. The father had become ill a year before, undergoing a serious and semi-successful operation and spending nine months in bed. To pay for the operation, they sold the *agrovila* house and their forty cows (a big herd for colonists). Now the family of eight was crammed into a mud house with two small bedrooms. They welcomed me as a guest for the weekend but not for a month. I insisted on paying but they would not take money. Like Sandman's family, who had allowed me to string up a hammock in the barn, this family had plenty of food and hospitality but no space. Dona Flora could think of no place on the side road where I could board for any length of time. Most families lived in the same cramped situation or worse. They would let me stay for a day or two, said Dona Flora, and they wouldn't let me pay, but nobody had room for a month.

In the three days I lived with the da Souzas, I found answers to many of the questions I was posing. Many answers came from the da Souzas' neighbor across the road, Alegre Vaisorte. The second night, Alegre and about thirty other people arrived at the house to watch Brazil play soccer against Venezuela on the da Souzas' television—a twelve-inch black and white set hooked to a car battery. Neighbors came up and down hills in the dark from six kilometers away for the game. Brazil destroyed Venezuela.

I spent the next day and a half interviewing Alegre. He was born in the early 1950s on a nearby river, long before any highways. When the highway came in 1970, he was in the middle of a seven-year stint hunting cats in the forest. He was the first of many to tell me, *Antes tinhamos onças demais*, "Before, we had cats galore." Soon after the cutting of the highway, his old profession came to an end in the region, he said. All the cats were dead and gone, hunted out of existence or scared away by the new colonists.

Alegre told me about family patterns in the region—who had moved on since 1970, who owned what. He noted that many of the earliest small farmer colonists had become medium or large farmers by buying other lots.

He told me how government policies and local society had changed over the decades. First of all, he said, INCRA had left. What INCRA had done previously, colonists did now for themselves (see Chapters 5 and 7). Frontier society had returned in many ways to what it had been before the 1950s and 1960s when colonists like his family built their own roads and bridges. Alegre then described how colonists had adapted their agricultural practices to the Amazon (see Chapters 4 and 5). He explained the properties of different soils I had seen and of some I hadn't seen and how they affected agricultural patterns. Patterns of planting and ownership emerged that I would soon detail with my questionnaire. He reminded me that the cacao I had seen in various parts of the road only grew in clay soils and that the wide-open pastures grew mostly on infertile sandy land. I asked him about a nearby lot that broke that pattern, having healthy pastures on fertile clay soils. He said that it was one of many lots owned by a single man. Large holders don't plant crops, he said. They just amass pasture and cattle.

Moran had told me about "entrepreneurial" small farmer colonists who bought several lots to become medium or large holders. Colonists don't really have a label for these entrepreneurs. Colonists refer to people occupying the 100-hectare lots along the highway as *colonos*, or colonists. They call those who own *glebas*—large farms of 500 to many thousands of hectares—*glebistas*. Colonists who own several lots blur the distinction between *colonos* and *glebistas*. The people Moran called "entrepreneurs" I will call "medium farmers." Colonists don't have a name for them.

People's attitudes toward me changed during the first few days I spent living with families on the side road. The first day I walked deep into the side road, a young girl spat on the ground and scowled to show her hostility toward me. Later that day, I greeted a boy of about fourteen as he rode past. He became spooked, along with his horse, and he dropped a sack of oranges as they galloped away. He would not return for the oranges until I turned and walked away. Fear of strangers is well-founded in a region where dead bodies dumped on the road are relatively common. I probably appeared stranger than most. However, after the first three days of living with families on the road and roaming around doing interviews, most people knew I was there, even if they weren't quite sure why. I ended up walking ten to twenty kilometers a day doing interviews on that road for most of the next month. By the end, kids and adults alike would join me for a kilometer or two of my walk, asking questions, chatting, and just being friendly.

Five days after walking onto the side road, I walked out with a good idea of where my research was heading. What I had observed on the trip to Sandman—the fallen and rebuilt bridge, soils, crops, open pastures, and forested areas—began making sense to me.

Side Road 27 served the objectives of my study. I wanted to determine how colonists had adapted their agricultural practices to different rainforest ecosystems. Colonists could work within the forest itself, but I surmised fairly quickly that colonists preferred to burn their forests. After the trees, the soils remain.

By comparing agricultural production on lots with different soil types, I could compare the colonists' adaptation strategies in different ecosystems. Side Road 27 has an unusually wide range of soils and terrains along with some very successful and some very poor farmers. Most side roads probably do not have as many wealthy farmers because many colonists on other side roads lack access to markets due to road closures. Side Road 27 is one of the few that is open to vehicle traffic from end to end throughout the year (the reasons for this will be discussed in chap. 7). It contained part of the settled community that Emilio Moran studied. He collected soil samples on many of the lots and has records of the original owners. I could use his information for comparison. Side Road 27 offered an ideal site for a longitudinal study of human interaction with the environment.

CIRA-PACAL

Having decided which side road I would sample, I traveled around to get a feel for the region. The Altamira-Médicilandia stretch of highway includes numerous *agrovilas*, a small administrative center known alternately as Brasil Novo or Kilometer 46, and a new municipal capital at Médicilandia, Kilometer 90 of the highway.

I used Nigel Smith's book, *Rainforest Corridors*, as a "Let's Go Transamazonia." He doesn't catalog outstanding eating establishments or even any reasonably priced bed-and-breakfasts, but he does mention some strange and interesting projects left over from the glory days of military rule. His book led me to Kilometer 92, where the giant steel tubing of a multimillion dollar sugar mill glitters against a green horizon.

Just outside Médicilandia stands a sugar refinery and a lumber mill. Both were built and run by INCRA. The refinery and mill are known as PACAL, the Projeto Agroindustrial Canaviera Abraham Lincoln (Agroindustrial Sugarcane Project at Agrovila Abraham Lincoln). Sugarcane producers, all colonists from the surrounding region, have formed a government-backed cooperative called CIRA, the Cooperativa Integral da Reforma Agraria (United Cooperative of the Agrarian Reform). So the project is known collectively as CIRA-PACAL. (Bureaucrats love acronyms.)

CIRA-PACAL offered an ideal place to study government-directed development for two reasons. One, it was the largest government project in the region. The operation includes over 270 independent sugarcane growers, a lumber mill, logging equipment (mostly bulldozers), and a refinery built at a cost of $6 million (in 1974 dollars). Two, I was able to befriend Rapaz, the on-site director of the project. He was twenty-two years old, liked beer, and had lived in New Jersey in 1985 during high school. Since I had passed through New Jersey that year looking at colleges, we were almost blood brothers. He was overjoyed to find someone his own age who could speak English in the middle of the Amazon. He provided me with relatively luxurious accommodations, presented extensive and not necessarily flattering information about the sugar and lumber project, and even gave me a grand tour. Rapaz's trust and help made the project easy to study.

Educated as a lawyer and intimately familiar with the bureaucracy in Brasília, he also explained some of the finer points of Brazilian politics and answered my questions on the new Brazilian Constitution.

I quickly learned of the nastier side of the CIRA-PACAL project through interviews with local skeptics, competing government agencies not receiving such favorable cash flows as the project, disgruntled members of the sugar cooperative, and the president of the local Rural Workers Union (one of the "Communists" in league with the priests and environmentalists, according to the union's detractors). The bustling regional center of Km. 92, with its class divisions and political factions, contrasted sharply with the sleepy community of Side Road 27.

The Bemvindo Family

When I returned to the Side Road 27 area, one family whom Emilio Moran and Alegre both had mentioned remained for me to contact—the Bemvindos. After leaving the PACAL project, I arrived at their house at dusk. After 6:00 p.m., traffic stops on the highway, and there is no way to get to town. Dona Linda, the matriarch, invited me to stay, and I ended up spending the next four weeks there. Since half of the family were either off on vacation or in the *garimpo* ("gold country") running a mining operation, they had plenty of room. I had a big bed in my own room in a wonderful home. When I needed privacy to work or just think, I could close the door, and they understood. They made me feel welcome, like family.

Among the first colonists to arrive in 1970, the Bemvindos had become the most successful farmers in the region. They owned three lots and had four houses on the family lot. The patriarch, Seu Melquiades, was both a political organizer and one of the most entrepreneurial farmers in the region. He pioneered Transamazonian cacao growing and constantly experimented with new crops. He has a more diverse farm than EMBRAPA, the nearby government agricultural research station, and is a leader in the Side Road 27 community and in regional affairs. Living with the Bemvindos and earning their respect and friendship put me in a strong position in local society.

In the twenty-five-year-old son, Christobal, I had a friend. He was a good farmer with knowledge of the local area, and he was somewhat cosmopolitan, having been educated in Altamira for nine years longer than the normal four-year grammar school education offered in the *agrovila*. Not being the patriarch, he was more removed from the political struggles of the region than his father, and he spoke with greater candor. We talked for hours almost every night.

Dona Linda loved to gossip, and this kind of information was a key to my understanding of local dynamics, not to mention being entertaining. The Bemvindos became my greatest source of information and support.

Every night the neighbors came to the house to watch television (the Bemvindos had three). Just by listening to the conversations and asking questions about things I did not understand or did not believe, I picked up valuable insights. This casual conversation served as a welcome change after eight- to twelve-hour days of formal interviews over questionnaires. On touchy subjects I usually turned to private conversations with Dona Linda, Seu Melquiades, or Christobal.

I employed different methods to approach different subjects. I briefly explored the traditional anthropological method of participant observation, in which the researcher gathers information by taking part in the activity being studied. On issues of the community, economy, infrastructure, and government, I surveyed the region much as a news reporter or a political scientist would—by visiting government agencies, talking to merchants, laborers, and landowners, and frequenting local restaurants and bars. Finally, with the questionnaires I gathered data on human interaction with the environment.

Interviews

Ethnoecology borrows from linguistics in that the researcher considers the informants to be the experts.[11] A culture, the linguists say, produces its own grammar and vocabulary. The various soil types I had learned about in class or books had their own names on the frontier and were defined, not necessarily by their pH levels or their potassium content, but by their textures and colors, and by what could grow in them (see chap. 4). I would have to learn the vocabulary of the colonists' world. I extended this approach from ethnoecology to economics and political science. Since I considered almost everyone to be an expert at something, I always had someone to interview. Most people liked being interviewed, because most people like being considered experts.

During interviews with the questionnaires, I tried to gather in the whole family. Mothers tended to know more about things such as education, ages, and numbers of children, while sons and daughters corrected their parents' faulty information. Most family members over the age of twelve (and sometimes much younger), male or female, work on the farm full time and are familiar with the production. With children and wives participating, interviews were more lively, also, as they broke apart the formal man to man setting which can feel like an interrogation. The questionnaires became family discussions.

The first few interviews using the questionnaires took a day or two with each family. By the fifteenth or twentieth interview, I spent only two hours with each family. By then I knew exactly what information I needed and was no longer confused by the agricultural terminology. Eventually, I developed a very practiced introduction and way of wording questions which allayed most fears and hesitations.

Sampling was not random. For reasons that will be discussed in Chapter 4, I tried to collect information on lots with all the different soil types that are represented on the side road. Since Side Road 27 has a fairly even distribution of soil types, I generally interviewed anyone I could find at home. If the owner and patriarch was not at home, I often walked around the farm to find him, or one of his kids went for me.

While I drew heavily from Moran and Smith in forming the questionnaires, I took my own direction once in the field. Colonists provided guidance for my study and influenced my final conclusions. Simple observations and simple events later had a profound impact on my study and thesis. With my time limited, I drew from only a few of the subject areas Moran and Smith studied and added subjects which the colonists find more pressing today. For example, the rise of collective action has become a major concern for colonists now. Twenty years ago, when Moran and Smith did their studies, collective action was floundering.

I dropped almost all questions concerning what colonists spent or earned. Questions on personal finances often seemed intrusive, while hyper-inflation and failing memories made real income or expenditures from past years difficult to estimate. Even if I could estimate personal income, it would not necessarily reflect the colonists' standard of living. Their lives are not entirely monetized. Colonists often barter for goods, and some produce solely cash crops while others produce more for subsistence. A farmer of cash crops may have a higher income but not eat as well as a subsistence farmer. The figures I do use are based only on prices current during the time I was there. Where significant, I provide probable price windows (highs and lows) for the year to account for variance during harvest. Estimating income or standard of living would demand methods far more complex and time consuming than those I used. My methods were simple, so my results are fairly simple.

I spent eight to twelve hours a day in formal interviews. Questioning continued with the Bemvindos on into the night. People became so used to me writing down what they said that some would pause with disapproving silence when I didn't write down something they considered important, so I wrote.

In addition to interviewing colonists, I interviewed individuals at numerous government agencies, including the regional directors of INCRA, CE-PLAC (Cacao Planning Commission), EMATER (rural credit assistance), and EMBRAPA (agriculture and cattle research agency). These men often had institutional memories stretching back to the days of highway building and the largesse granted to bureaucrats under the military regime. Many bemoaned the bureaucracy's present state of disrepair. With some, I found that time spent with underlings was much more informative on most points because the directors often practiced fairly blatant political deception, from gentle bending of the truth to brutal twisting. I spoke with the presidents of the Rural Workers Unions at both Km. 90 and Altamira, as well as current and former members. I visited two agricultural research stations, one run by EMBRAPA that researched a variety of products (rubber, Brazil nuts, rice, beans, cacao) and the other run by the sugar cooperative that researched only sugarcane.

Limitations

Experts are not always truthful. I felt that people were lying to me in several instances and exaggerating or avoiding the truth in others. Usually I let the subject drop in such cases. I would note it in my head and ask another informant the same question to see whether that answer confirmed or denied the first. I left questionable information out of the analysis, unless I found people bending the truth consistently, which indicated an issue that held some significance and was worth covering up. This was the case most often with government technicians and bureaucrats, who were universally helpful in interviews but not necessarily truthful. Sometimes farmers seemed to invent numbers for crop yields to please me. They might have had no idea of how much rice they had produced that year but would give me a number. As a result, I found most reports on yields so untrustworthy or incomplete that I will not use them to estimate production.

Gender certainly affected my research. I studied agriculture and politics, spheres dominated by men in this frontier society. The fact that I was male enabled me to speak openly and research comfortably in these spheres; I could not enter the world of women so easily. A separation of sexes exists on the frontier akin to the nineteenth century "cult of domesticity" in the United States. As a result, I largely omitted the "domestic" sphere from my study.[12] This placed limits on agroeconomics research. For example, although I did collect extensive data on labor, I cannot give an accurate analysis of labor here because men often ignored the hours put in by women until directly questioned, and even then they were sometimes evasive. Women and children are not supposed to work by traditional standards, but they do—especially during harvest when the work is not backbreaking but is essential and time-consuming. More dangerous and strenuous work, like deforesting, is apparently done exclusively by men. Not surprisingly, government agencies gave labor estimates for agriculture in *man*-days per year. From casual observation, I can say that men who live alone on a farm without any women may survive, but they do not live well. Even if they make a lot of money, men whose wives and families live apart from them in Altamira generally live like paupers: unkempt and poorly fed.[13]

Generally, I tried not to pressure people or trap them; if they felt something was not my business, that was their right. I strongly believe that some questions and some photography violate people's privacy. Certain things belong in novels, not in academic works. My own ethical qualms about areas considered "kosher" in traditional anthropology also placed limits on this study.

The opinions of my Amazonian family, the Bemvindos, heavily influenced my final conclusions, and I continually discussed my research with them. Most of the time they corroborated the information I gathered and agreed with my conclusions. This was no accident. Almost all of the information I gathered and present here is common knowledge to the well-informed farmer. How one interprets that information is open to debate. The Bemvindos hold what I consider to be forward-thinking views from an ecological standpoint, while we share similar political and social values. In

Little Bemvindos: future farmers of Amazonia hang out on the porch.

my travels through Asia, Europe, and Latin America, nowhere else have I felt so at home. They were the experts I trusted most.

Though it seemed to open many doors, my living situation with the Bemvindos probably limited the information I received in some cases. This became obvious only once, when two parties (the Bemvindos being one) tried to make me a pawn in their battle over some land. They both wanted to know what the other was thinking, so they both gave me their sides of the story. I pleaded the Fifth to all parties: no information for either side. They allowed me to leave the battle zone quietly. The incident provided valuable insights into social relations on the frontier, as well as practical information such as current prices for land at a time when virtually no one could sell property.

The biggest drawback of living with the Bemvindos was location. The family lives on the main highway, five kilometers away from Side Road 27. This meant I didn't actually live in the community I studied. I could always hitchhike on the highway but rarely on Side Road 27, so I walked in and out daily. Seu Melquiades' tractor was one of the few vehicles that made the twenty-kilometer trip to the end of the side road where he owned two other lots. I joined him for a few days to stay with some of his relatives in order to do interviews back there.

How did the colonists view me? Foreign ecologists have a dubious reputation in some circles in the Amazon. Sting, the musician, and many other American and European *ecologistas* had recently (winter 1989) taken part in a massive demonstration in Altamira against a proposed hydroelectric dam soon to flood much of the nearby area around the Xingu River. The dam would be the largest ever built in a rainforest and one of the largest in the world. Originally, the government had named the dam project "Kararaô" after the Native American tribe whose lands it would flood. The name was later dropped. The project is extremely controversial within Brazil; the arrival of foreign ecologists antagonized proponents of the dam and made local people acutely aware of the global concerns over their region.

Once, a passerby saw me talking to some folks in town, listened in very briefly, then accused me of being an *ecologista*, "like Sting and the Indians," trying to take the colonists' land and their livelihood away from them. "No," I explained, showing him my questionnaire, "I'm an *agronomista* ["agronomist"], but I do care about ecology and the best way to use resources, just like you do." This brought nods of approval from other colonists and begrudging acceptance from him. I shaped my study of agro-economics knowing that *ecologistas* are not welcome in many households. *Agronomistas* are. From the colonists' perspective, *agronomistas* are scientists, *ecologistas* are ideologues. I did not hide my concerns over deforestation and environmental destruction, though I did couch them in friendly terms.

Only once did I meet with open hostility, from a colonist I was interviewing on Side Road 27. In this case I explained more carefully the provisions outlined in my Human Subjects speech, repeating that if he did not want to be interviewed or answer any questions, he did not have to do so. He said he understood and was willing to answer questions. I then hurriedly finished the interview, figuring that that was the price one paid as a researcher for intruding on people's lives. His wife was somewhat apologetic for the treatment. I apologized for the inconvenience.

I worried about how the colonists perceived me and once asked Dona Linda what she thought. *Te gustam*, she said, they like you. She told me the story of some *Paulistas* (people from São Paulo) who had come with a television crew for a few days to do a story on successful Amazonian small farmers. The crew stayed in the most expensive hotel in Altamira and acted like peacocks, she said. When she offered them a glass of water on the hot afternoon they arrived, they refused, afraid of contracting some disease. They seemed to disdain the Amazonian way of life—as *caboclo* living. She said from that point on she offered them nothing—no coffee, no food, not even a chair. I drank their water, went hunting and fishing with them, sat around for conversations over coffee, and lived with them. Although I felt I would always be an outsider, they accepted me as a temporary member of the community in my capacity as a researcher.

In the first week, as I adjusted to language differences and a totally new environment, I sometimes played the idiot. When I said, "I don't get it," people explained things in more detail. The more they tried to explain the obvious, the more they provided the beliefs and assumptions behind the words they commonly use. *Sem terras* means "without lands" in Portuguese. But "landless" can have negative connotations on the frontier, much like "homeless" has negative connotations in America. Language lessons became research opportunities. Colonists come from all parts of the country—the South, the Northeast, and the Amazon. Learning the language was something like trying to learn English while moving among Irish, Italian, and African-American neighborhoods in New York City at the turn of the century. A local accent has emerged, but colonists revert to their regional dialects when they are with people from their own region. Once I could speak with them on their terms, using Amazonian idioms or farm terminology, I gained a reputation for having some intelligence.

In addition, by coming there alone, hitchhiking, and walking around unarmed, they thought me bold, if not a little nutty. Generally, I was treated with a great deal of respect. Usually this respect, which was mutual, helped foster discussion. In a few instances, respect became deference, a barrier which made an interview seem like a formal meeting rather than a relaxed discussion.

All in all, I met many wonderful people, almost all of whom were very hospitable. I left the house every morning with a bottle of water, a notebook, and a camera and arrived back at sunset. People offered me lunch and water refills throughout the day. I never asked for food, but only once did I miss lunch. Their care and generosity always amazed me.

4

CASTLES IN THE SAND

After the trees in Amazonia, a sloth peers out from the forest's edge at a wide open field of smoking stumps. Primeval instinct for canopy protection stops the animal from crossing open spaces. Though its old forest home and feeding grounds lie only a few hundred meters across the field, the sloth will die on this side of the chasm without ever crossing again. After the trees, unbroken forests become an archipelago of island ecosystems.

Colonists and the Amazonian Ecosystem

Deforesting is not something colonists do for kicks; it's a nasty business. When I met Alegre, he had a swollen foot and was taking antibiotics after an over-zealous chop with a machete went not only through the branch he intended to cut but also through his thick rubber boot and a good way into his foot. Sandman's foot had recently been crushed by a falling log. The patriarch of the Bemvindo family, Seu Melquiades, had a large scar between his eyes and was missing part of his nose. While he was felling trees in the 1970s, his chainsaw jumped and hit him in the face. That was the last time he, himself, deforested. Now he, like most of the older farmers in the region, prefers to hire laborers, usually landless young men, to do the deforesting since it is so dangerous. Trees are even more dangerous than the chainsaws. Much of the Altamira region has a forest type called *mata de cipó*, which translates best as a "vine forest" or liana forest. The vines make the forest look like a tangled web, with each tree attached to all the surrounding trees. If the deforester cuts down one tree, the tree behind him may be pulled down on his head as he watches the one he cut fall down in front of him. Not a pleasant job. So why do they do it?

Continued Amazonian deforestation results partially from social and economic pressures discussed earlier that exclude colonists from the agriculturally settled regions of the country. However, deforestation is also the product of certain aspects of the Amazonian ecosystem. Once colonists clear and plant an area for crops or pasture, soil fertility drops precipitously, and yields decline. Heavy rains wash away soils no longer protected by forest cover. Poor soils and rapid erosion create a pattern of continued deforestation and, as cleared areas become worn out, onward migration.

Soil infertility emerged as a primary pressure toward onward migration and continued deforestation. While large landholders have come to control the overwhelming majority of ranchlands, colonist small farmers have been blamed for much of the burning. Hecht and Cockburn state that colonists clear the land as subsistence-speculators, raise crops until soil fertility drops, then sell the land as pasture to medium or large cattle interests.[1] That small farmers do not remain on cleared land to continue farming is hardly surprising: more than 80 percent of the soils in the Amazon are acidic infertile sand, making them difficult for most forms of agriculture.[2] Grass is one of the few plants that survives on such soils once they have been stripped of their rich forest cover.

Colonists have actually settled permanently in the Altamira region, breaking the pattern of continued migration described by Hecht and Cockburn. The most recent migrant I found had purchased his lot three years earlier, in 1986. Initially, 80 percent or more of the farmers migrated on during the first five years of colonization (1970–1975) and fewer than 10 percent of the original colonists remain on their lots. Yet those who do remain and those who have settled since appear to be a very stable, self-selected group of hard working, fairly successful small and medium holding farmers. In many ways, the area is no longer a frontier but a settled community. Since the farmers I interviewed hope their children will raise crops on their same plot of land, they consider long-term sustainability as well as short-term profits in their agricultural decisions. This chapter addresses soil quality as a primary concern for colonist farmers in agricultural decision making.

Deforestation and Human Adaptation to the Ecosystem

The soils and terrain covering much of the region are simply unfavorable for the intensive agricultural techniques the colonists introduced. According to Nigel Smith, "The Transamazon [Highway] was clearly not designed to provide access to the best soils of Amazonia."[3] The highway cut across great expanses of nutrient-poor, acidic sands. These are marginal for agriculture by almost any standard. Once colonists had cut down and burned the trees, and the rains had washed away their nutrient-rich ash, the colonists realized that these rainforests had been glorious green castles in the sand. The question of how luxuriant rainforests can thrive on seemingly hostile soils has captivated botanists while confounding colonists. Soil, more than any other factor, has shaped the patterns of small holder colonist agriculture.

Of the three major tropical regions in the world—Asia, Africa, and Latin America—the latter is notorious for having the worst soils. Table 4.1 introduces soil distribution in the humid tropics globally, indicating some major constraints to agriculture in humid tropical America. These are rough estimates and sources disagree on the numbers since no comprehensive survey has been taken of Amazonian soils. Even as rough estimates, they bode poorly for Amazonian agriculturalists. As table 4.1 reveals, 81 percent of humid tropical America—as opposed to 56 percent of humid tropical Africa and 38 percent of humid tropical Asia—has acidic soils with low native fertility.[4] Add to that the very infertile sandy areas along with the shallow and poorly drained areas, and Amazonia is left with less than 10 percent of its land suitable for intensive cultivation. How colonists have adapted their agricultural practices to such soils and the implications that their adaptations hold for future colonization forms the subject of this and the next chapter.

One might think that acidic infertile soils would mitigate forest growth, but constant tropical heat and humidity create an ideal climate for plants, animals, and insects. Whereas temperate forests rely on nutrients stored in the soil, rainforests rely on recycling their own organic material for nutrients. Rainforests in infertile areas feed not on the soils but on themselves (see fig. 4.1).

Rainforest structures vary just as rainforest species do. Forests within walking distance of Side Road 27 have seemingly opposite structures. Two major forest types grow in the Altamira region: *mata de cipó* and mature

Table 4.1. *General Distribution of the Main Types of Soils in the Humid Tropics*

General Soil Grouping	Humid Tropical America (%)	Humid Tropical Africa (%)	Humid Tropical Asia and Pacific (%)	World's Humid Tropics (%)
1. Acidic, low native fertility soils (Oxisols, Ultisols, Dystropepts)	81	56	38	63
2. Very infertile sandy soils (Psamments, Spodosols)	2	16	6	7
3. Poorly drained soils (Aquepts)	6	12	6	8
4. Shallow soils (Lithic Entosols)	3	3	10	5
5. Moderately fertile, well-drained soils (Alfisols, Vertisols, Mollisols, Andepts, Tropepts, Fluvents)	7	12	33	15
6. Organic Soils (Histosols)	1	1	6	2
Total	100	100	100	100

Source: Moran 1990: 130, adapted from Sanchez 1987.

upland forests. In mature upland forests, one can often walk upright in clear space because little vegetation grows near the ground. In *mata de cipó*, the vines, spines, trees, and shrubs growing near the forest floor make foot travel difficult without a machete.[5]

Mature upland forests have a closed canopy structure. The canopy effectively filters sun and rain. Shade impedes plant growth on the forest floor, leaving the area near the ground relatively open. Those life-forms that convert sunlight to energy through photosynthesis must live up in the canopy to receive sun at all. Forest creatures that eat such plants also live in the canopy. As a result, upper branches of the enormous hardwood trees literally crawl with life—epiphytes, arachnids, insects, sloths, snakes, frogs, monkeys, birds, and fungi. If leaves fall from the trees, they may be caught

Tropical soils do not compare well with soils in temperate climates. Many soils in the temperate regions were churned up or deposited by glaciers during the last ice age and have been weathered only since ice flows receded 12,000 years ago. As a result, soils in temperate regions contain newly replenished nutrient reserves. Soils underneath tropical forests have undergone millions of years of weathering with heavy rainfall. Heavy rains wash nutrients deep below the surface or into streams and rivers. Whereas temperate forests rely on nutrient reserves in the soils themselves, tropical forests store nutrients in biomass. The forest canopy protects topsoil from direct exposure to sun, wind, and rain.

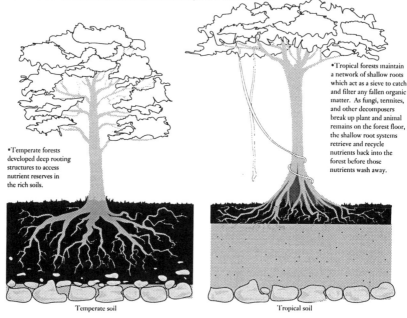

•Tropical forests maintain a network of shallow roots which act as a sieve to catch and filter any fallen organic matter. As fungi, termites, and other decomposers break up plant and animal remains on the forest floor, the shallow root systems retrieve and recycle nutrients back into the forest before those nutrients wash away.

•Temperate forests developed deep rooting structures to access nutrient reserves in the rich soils.

Temperate soil   Tropical soil

Figure 4.1: Forest, roots, and soil structures in the rainforest.

and converted into food by plants covering the branches below. If plant or animal debris does reach the forest floor, it is reclaimed by the extensive root system and by insects, bacteria, and fungi before its nutrients are lost into the acidic soils, then washed into streams and rivers by the constant rains. The forest thereby conserves and recycles virtually all of its nutrients.

When one of the large trees falls, it brings down all the plants and animals on and around it. The "gap" in the canopy enables sunlight to hit the forest floor, and those plant species that had been effectively shaded are now able to seed.[6] The forest quickly recolonizes the open area, taking up the nutrients left by the dying tree and its coterie of plants and animals. Thus the forest perpetuates itself in a closed nutrient cycle.

Actually, the nutrient cycle is not quite closed. With such a paucity of nutrients in the soils, where did the forest find the nutrients for its genesis?

Perhaps out of thin air. Scientists believe Amazonian rainforests may feed on African soils. Michael Garstang and Robert Swap, studying soil loss in Africa, have found that winds carry soils away as dust from arid regions of Africa—Angola, Namibia, South Africa, and the Sahara—and deposit those soils in tropical storms over Amazonia, the Caribbean, and Florida. They estimate that during each rainy season "the eastern Amazon receives more than 13 million tons of dust with vital nutrients, including phosphates, which speed plant growth."[7] They found evidence of African soils as far inland as Manaus. As Africa loses its topsoil, the Americas reap the reward. Robert Talbot, a member of the same research team as Garstang and Swap, argues that South American rainforests have expanded and contracted with the expansion and contraction of African deserts. Their research debunks the myth of the Amazon as a self-contained, self-sufficient ecosystem.[8]

Biologists once spoke of ecosystems in "equilibrium," where all the components of an ecosystem balanced each other. Rainforests may have seemed the greatest example of such an equilibrium, their incredible "web of life"

Pets of the forest: these parrots landed as fledglings, along with their tree, when this farmer was felling forests for agriculture on Side Road 27. Parrots can be both pets and crop pests for Amazonian farmers.

so tautly spun that every little creature and every tree kept the balance and maintained the web. However, the concept of ecosystems in equilibrium is somewhat archaic. Rainforests change constantly with species evolving and dying out. This incredible flux is largely responsible for the diversity found in rainforests. But the analogy of a web does illuminate one aspect of rainforest ecology—destroy one part of the web, and the whole is affected.

Soils and forests all over the Amazon show signs of human occupation and human tinkering. The Amazon once held within its forests great populations that utilized the biodiversity. Only careful forest and soil management could sustain such populations. Geographer Nigel Smith and ethnobotanist Bill Balée argue that *mata de cipó* forests resulted from Native American occupation and manipulation. Colonists often refer to the liana forests as covering the most fertile soils of the region.

Smith notes that protruding Brazil nut trees are common in liana forests, while other emergent tree species are less frequent. Brazil nuts were a significant source of protein for Native Americans in the region. Smith also reports reduced biomass and species diversity in *mata de cipó* without a discernible drop in game yields.[9] This might indicate that indigenous people fostered the growth of Brazil nuts and game yields by managing second growth. Essentially, these liana forests are mature second growth forests— not to be confused with mature upland primary forests. Smith attributes the structure of liana forests to "a disclimax caused by millennia of felling and burning by aborigines."[10] A reduced species diversity, even after hundreds of years of forest recovery, bodes poorly for newly colonized areas ever regaining the biodiversity of primary forests.

Swidden Techniques

Humankind has tinkered with the web for thousands of years by managing the forests in a swidden (cutting and burning) system. Though long considered simple and "primitive," indigenous agricultural techniques that employ swidden methods can actually be quite sophisticated. Traditional swidden methods of farming imitate the gap dynamics of mature forests and maintain the nutrient cycle. Swidden agriculturalists cut down only small areas of one-half to one hectare to plant crops. By burning the plot, they turn forest biomass into a nutrient rich ash that is then taken up by crops. The burn also kills seeds and seedlings in the ground so that the forest does not recolonize the area quite so quickly. Such plots prevent significant erosion since they are small, surrounded by forest, and covered in fallen trees which anchor the soils.

Swidden agriculturalists plant a wide variety of cultivars, rather than a monoculture, that utilizes different nutrients and that is resistant to various insects, fungi, and animals.[11] Amazonians have compensated for poor soils by planting crops such as manioc that grow well in infertile soils. When soil nutrients become so exhausted that yields drop or when the plot becomes choked by weeds and secondary forest growth, swidden farmers allow the surrounding forests to recolonize the area, thereby minimizing long-term degradation.[12]

At this point, swidden agriculturalists don't simply abandon the plot. Dominique Irvine, an ecological anthropologist who studied the Runa of the Ecuadoran Amazon, redefined swidden, calling it the "first stage of a larger agroforestry management system."[13] Many Amazonian indigenous peoples manage the forest continually—from felling the trees to the forest's maturation. As the forest regrows, swidden farmers encourage the species that are beneficial to humankind.

Indigenous and forest peoples then engage in extractive industries, culling valuable products that they planted or protected, such as fruits, nuts, medicines, herbs, rubber, and building materials. *Açaí* palm farmers on the *várzea* provide one of the best examples of successful forest management. Instead of deforesting and planting monocultural orchards, they maintain the forest structure and biodiversity while increasing the number of *açaí* trees in the area.[14] They do so by thinning the number of naturally growing tree species and replacing them with *açaí*. The palms do well under canopy shade since that is their natural habitat. Unlike slash and burn monoculturalists, *açaí* palm farmers depend on the forest structure to maintain their harvest. The same holds true for certain species of favorites such as coffee and cacao. Coffee in the Dominican Republic and cacao in Western Pará are both grown under the canopy of managed forests.

Forest management has been practiced in the Amazon quite probably as long as humankind has occupied the region. As a result, according to ethnobotanist Bill Balée, at least 11.8 percent, and probably much more, of Brazil's Amazonian *terra firme* forests and soils are anthropogenic.[15] In other words, the so-called virgin forests of the Amazon either once were or still are carefully managed to maximize their benefit to humankind. To forest peoples, the forest is not some untamed jungle (as it was perceived by nine-teenth century European explorers and twentieth century development-minded planners), but a manicured and productive garden.

Lest one think that a garden makes a poor substitute for a diverse rain-forest, consider the practices of the Kayapó tribe of the Upper Xingu River. Research on the Kayapó suggests that indigenous peoples' forest manage-ment actually contributed to the biodiversity of the Amazon. The Kayapó select the best species for their needs from a region the size of France. Taking full advantage of the Amazon's incredible gene pool, they introduce these species into their swidden plots.[16] As canopy cover returns, the Ka-yapó continue to harvest fruits, vines, medicinal plants, and animals that thrive in the managed forests. The Kayapó are not unusual. Native "gar-dens" were so complex and diverse that until recently few researchers even considered that the forests might be anthropogenic.

Most swidden systems depend on low population densities and tremen-dous forest reserves to provide long fallow periods, thus allowing forests to recover and their species and nutrients to rejuvenate. These methods proved sustainable for thousands of years in the Amazon, as indicated by the healthy forests at which highway builders arrived in 1970. By imitating the gap and succession cycles of the forest, swidden systems alter, but do not annihilate, the forest ecosystem. Swidden farmers and forest managers might be thought of as eco-tinkerers.

Colonization and Intensive Agriculture

The scale and sheer incompetence of recent human "tinkering" as a result of colonization of the Amazon has altered the ecosystem in dramatic and unexpected ways. Almost uniformly, colonist land management over the last twenty years has not even approached the complexity of ancient swid-den systems.[17] Colonists and cattle ranchers deforest and burn much larger areas and permanently maintain those areas under intensive agriculture. In effect, their open landscapes create new island ecosystems within the rain-forest ecosystem. In a mature forest, species check each other's growth so that no single species dominates. When their canopy is destroyed and many of those species are burned, species that can survive in the new unshaded, intensive agricultural environment go unchecked by their former predators or competitors. Humankind then renames the hardy survivors "pests." Colonist deforestation has torn the biological web.

For example, mosquitoes generally live in the forest's upper canopy, feeding on monkeys, sloths, and other juicy creatures. The mosquitoes are, in turn, eaten by predators such as birds and bats. When humans radically alter the ecosystem by deforesting, in addition to wiping out many predator species, they create new breeding and feeding grounds for some of the more adaptive species, like mosquitoes. Felling trees brings mosquitoes to ground- and people-level. Rain which had been absorbed by the forest may now lie in pools of stagnant water.

Incidence of malaria rapidly increases in areas where massive deforestation is occurring, as along the highway during the 1970s and 1980s.[18] Colonists themselves brought malaria in their blood to the Amazon from other parts of Brazil; *Anopheles darlingi* mosquitoes then spread the disease to other colonists.[19] In addition, colonists have taken to damming rivers and building lakes for fisheries and small hydroelectric projects. Lakes provide even larger breeding areas for mosquitoes. As a result, incidence of malaria is on the rise again in the zone around the lakes, especially among people who fish for subsistence. One of the little *Anopheles* tyrants sunk his snout into me, probably when I was fishing, according to my nurse in Belém. Malaria has a fifteen- to twenty-five-day incubation period in the body, and I came down with the fever after leaving the region. Smith reports that "between 5 and 25 percent of the Transamazon residents contract malaria every year."[20] Malaria incapacitates a person for weeks or months with fevers and intolerable headaches. The disease can dramatically reduce a family's ability to feed itself if one or more working members are afflicted.

The mosquito is one example of the many changes humankind has wrought in Amazonia. Like the *Anopheles* mosquito, insects and fungi that can survive on crops when rid of their former predators and competitors are checked only by their appetites and by whatever insecticides and fungicides colonists can afford. Heavy rains wash away chemicals, so chemical manufacturers recommend repeated applications for effectiveness. With repeated chemical applications, the "pests" develop resistance even to those toxins. Colonist alterations of the biological web by the introduction of intensive agriculture has led to an increasing frequency of attacks by insects, animals, and fungi on crops, as discussed in the following chapter. The same climatological conditions of heat and humidity that help foster rainforest biodiversity create nightmares for colonist agriculture.

In addition to the biological changes colonists have wrought on their ecosystem, deforestation can result in dramatic hydrological shifts. In

Sunset on a forest cemetery: damming a creek created this lake, which flooded twelve hectares of forest and killed these trees. The lake provides fish for the nearby *agrovila*, along with breeding grounds for mosquitoes that carry malaria. Larger hydroelectric projects flood thousands of acres throughout Amazonia.

mature rainforests, moisture is "recycled" on the order of 50 percent through evapotranspiration.[21] Rainforests act as great evapotranspiring sponges. With rain, the forests soak up water; with sun, the forest sponge is squeezed, and half that water turns from droplets on leaves and moisture in plants back into mists, into the atmosphere, and into more rainfall. The other half remains under the canopy, keeping the forest relatively cool and moist. Yet the hydrological cycle is delicate and easily altered. Large-scale deforestation removes the sponge. Rather than being recycled within the region, rains are washed over barren fields, into the rivers, and out to the ocean. "Old-timers" in the Altamira region speak of the 1950s when it rained ten months out of the year. Today, six months of rain per year are more common. Rainfall varies throughout the Amazon, and both wet and dry years are not uncommon. As no consistent rainfall data was collected prior to highway construction, we simply do not know the long-term hydrological effects of colonization. Mists that formerly would have been absorbed by the forest now hover over deforested areas in the early morning but are gone with the day's sun. Ground-level temperatures rise dramatically in unshaded fields. Hecht and Cockburn report that temperatures in Amazonian pastures are 10 to 20 degrees Fahrenheit above those of the forest.[22] Drying of the Amazon will likely contribute to a change in the global heat balance. How this will affect global warming is any supercomputer's guess.

Erosion emerged early on as a major agroecological consequence of colonization. Whereas swidden farmers use small plots, colonists clear large areas; while swidden farmers leave fallen logs on the ground to anchor the soil and prevent erosion, colonists often remove them. Widespread deforestation strips the land of its natural protection. Consequently, colonized areas suffer from extensive erosion.

I encountered the effects of catastrophic soil erosion everywhere and actually watched it happen while leaving the municipal center of Médicilandia. The town perches on the southeastern slope of a hill. The main street is wide to accommodate all the horses, trucks, buses, and tractors passing daily. Until the last day of my stay, the rich clay street baked under the dry-season sun—four weeks with no rain. Every shop, every vehicle, every body in town was bathed in reddish dust. As I walked out of town that afternoon, hitching a ride to Altamira, clouds formed and the rains began—first drizzle, then a torrential onslaught. Within minutes the dust turned to cascading mud. Layer after layer of thick purple streams careened down the hill. Streams formed gullies, and gullies became small chasms down the middle of the road. Every road I had seen in the Amazon had these gullies, but I had never realized how suddenly and violently they were created. This road had no protection from the sun or rains.

Degraded pastures offer little protection. The nutrients that are pulled literally from the sky over millions of years can wash away in a matter of days or even hours under this deluge. Recovery will be long in coming. With the present magnitude of nutrient loss, some areas may never recover.

Disease, erosion, and changes in local hydrology form only part of the larger ecosystemic change. One final and foreboding addendum to this deforestation story: the burn itself contributes to global warming. When colonists set fire to deforested areas, much of the forest biomass belches into the atmosphere as carbon dioxide, adding greenhouse gasses by the millions of tons.[23] As Allen Savory states, "The world as we know it is at stake. Global warming may well bring the ultimate desert to all of us, and

Road to ruin: an erosion ditch splits Side Road 27—a mere two years' worth of damage. Weed and palm tree invasion in the pasture on the left and white patches of sand along the fence indicate overgrazing and degradation. Deforestation strips the soils of protection from heavy rains, and massive erosion plagues the region, even on the relatively flat ground shown here.

yet we will not stop it until we recognize it as a matter of the mineral cycle and succession. Cutting emissions is certainly necessary, but it really only buys time. Even if we succeed, we'll be a bit like firemen congratulating ourselves on getting the flames in the attic down to three feet high and calling it a day, wouldn't we? The carbon we've pumped into the air was locked up in organic matter over vast periods of geologic time. It won't go away until it is returned to that form."[24] Forest peoples have been burning forests for millennia, but never on today's order of magnitude, and their plots always returned to forest. Whatever their burning put into the atmosphere would be taken up again through "the mineral cycle and succession." What had been a mineral cycle has become a downward spiral.

In the initial stages of colonization, colonists had enough mature forest reserves to cut and burn new areas for every crop. Colonists deforested areas first for agriculture, then maintained them as pasture once the burned forest nutrients had been exhausted. Within one to three years of continued cropping in one area, yields on poor soils rapidly declined. Grass survived for another ten years on a deforested area, maybe, then the land became too degraded from erosion, nutrient leaching, and soil compaction to support even that. With time, colonists were forced to allow the forest to recover somewhat in order for the land to produce anything at all. Their lots were soon covered in pasture and secondary growth (known as *capoeira*), and they were running out of forest reserves.

If we take "ecological sustainability as a rough index of management success," as ethnoecologist Berkes and his colleagues argue, the colonists' agricultural system proved unsuccessful rather quickly.[25] Moran and Smith witnessed the beginnings of a crisis in soil fertility. Even when Moran and Smith had looked on, much of the forest had fallen, and the topsoil had washed away between blades of pasture grass. Both researchers pointed to soils as a long-term limiting factor in regional development.

Colonists' conceptions of development are rooted in the soil. By clearing and tilling the land, they redirect the ecosystem's energy toward human consumption. Whereas swidden agriculture relies on forest nutrients for fertility, intensive agriculture relies on nutrients stored in the soils themselves or on those provided by additives and correctives. Due to declining fertility after forest biomass is removed, soil properties become essential over time in intensive agriculture. At the time of Moran's and Smith's studies, few of the colonists knew much about Amazonian soil types, but they were beginning to realize how significantly soils and terrain factored into productivity. Unfortunately for colonists, the lush forest cover of the Amazon hides some of the poorest soils on the planet. An understanding of frontier agricultural development, therefore, begins with understanding frontier soils.

On my first walk down Side Road 27, I realized how little I understood what "heterogeneous soils" meant. Beneath the myriad kinds of forest lie many types of soils and terrain. Here might be white sand (*areia branca*), there some mixed soils of sand and clay (*terra mixta*), and over the hill a patch of purple clay (*terra roxa*). In effect, these pockets of different soils define their own little ecosystems. Different plant species thrive in each type of soil; different animals and insects survive on those plants. The diversity of soils quite probably contributes to the diversity of the Amazon rainforest.[26]

Diverse soils also favor a patchwork of different kinds of agriculture. That patchwork is predictable if one knows where different soils lie as well as what cultivars thrive in various soil types. I found that agricultural patterns have emerged to reflect the quality of soils in the region. These patterns have implications for the social distribution of land.

Soil Classification Systems

In the field I relied on colonists' descriptions of soils and will use their classification system in this chapter. Academic discussions of soils can become extremely technical. Like many other academicians, geographers and soil ecologists make their living by being precise. This often makes their work obscure and inaccessible to the average reader or colonist, as Nigel Smith demonstrates when describing soils in the Altamira region:

> Podzolic soils (ultisols), usually well drained with an accumulation of clay in the B horizon, are particularly common on the Pre-Cambrian granitic shield and account for 41 percent of the soils in the colonized zone. . . . [Podzolics are] generally strongly acid with a low cation exchange capacity.[27]

A colonist might describe the same soils simply as *areia mixta* or *terra fraca*, "mixed sand" or "weak soils."

Colonists classify soils by what they look and feel like, by their sand and clay content, by their nutrients, and by the kinds of crops, plant species, and forests the soils can support. Based on their experience, colonists cre-

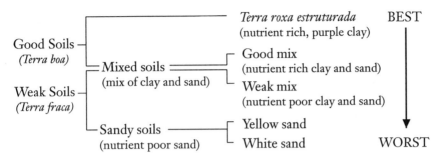

Figure 4.2: Colonists' soil classification system.

ated a taxonomy of the soils in their area, shown in fig. 4.2. Colonists use progressively more complex classifications. They divide *terra boa* (good soils) and *terra fraca* (weak soils) into three categories: *terra roxa, terra mixta* (mixed soils), and *terra de areia* (sandy soils). (I use direct translations of their designations.) I will be using terms in the far right column of the figure to describe colonist land use.

1. *Terra roxa* (pronounced "terra ro-sha") translates as "purple earth" and is exactly that. The reddish purple soil, as described earlier, is rich in nutrients with a high clay content. *Terra roxa* is rare in the Amazon (constituting up to 7 percent of the land), but concentrations of it are fairly common on the stretch of highway from Altamira to about 140 kilometers east, making those areas some of the rarest but most valuable agricultural land in the Amazon.
2. Mixed soils are a mix of sand and clay. Based on whether the soil is nutrient rich or poor, acidic or neutral, colonists classify mixed soils as either
   a. Good mix (a fertile mix of clay and sand)
   b. Weak mix (an infertile mix of clay and sand, usually acidic).
3. Sandy soils, the third designation, are considered the worst for agriculture. Sands are classified by their color,
   a. Yellow sand
   b. White sand.[28]
4. "Several" is a category I have added to describe lots with some combination of the soil types above. For example, a lot might be mostly white sand but have pockets of good mix. No "several soil" exists; lots with several soil types are common.

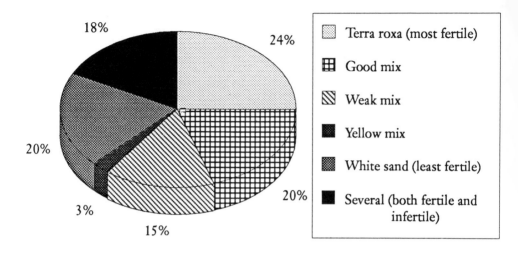

18%   24%

☐ Terra roxa (most fertile)

⊞ Good mix

◩ Weak mix

■ Yellow mix

▨ White sand (least fertile)

20%

■ Several (both fertile and infertile)

20%

3%

15%

Figure 4.3: Soil types and their general fertility (*N* = 40).

As stated earlier, I chose Side Road 27 because of the extreme heterogeneity of its soils. According to colonists, all the soils of the region are represented on this road. Figure 4.3 gives a breakdown (by percentage of lots) of the different soil types I encountered in my study.

The pie chart of soils is based on a forty lot sample (i.e., 4,000 hectares or 40 square kilometers), including lots designated as "secondary lots." The following analysis will use four colonist designations in their order of fertility: *terra roxa*, good mix, weak mix, and white sand. I found no yellow sand on "primary lots" and will not use this soil type in the analysis. According to colonists, it produces crops just like the infertile white sand. I have added the category of "several" to denote lots with extremely diverse soils that are farmed accordingly. Generally these lots had poorer soil qualities with pockets of nutrient rich soils—often alluvial soils deposited on the edges of creeks. In a few instances the lots designated as "several" had significant amounts of good soil.

Colonists' understanding of soils went well beyond these basic classifications. The more I asked for clarification, the more complex their descriptions became. This one is good mix, a colonist once said, when it looked like the same white sand that another colonist had called weak soil. No, he said: this area has twenty centimeters of white sand atop a meter of white, sandy clay that is fairly fertile and below that is several meters of purple clay, *terra roxa*. He showed me to a well that his sons were digging with the different layers of soil now visible down the walls of the well. Each layer had a different texture and sand/clay content. On this area of his lot, the sand had good drainage, but the plants relied on the more fertile under-soils for nutrients. Other areas of his lot were not as rich, he said. Such complex understanding of the ecosystem comes from their direct and con-tinued experience in working with the land.

Colonists know not only the soils in areas they have deforested and planted, but also the quality of soils over their entire lots. Certain plants within a forest denote certain soil qualities. Colonists believe *babaçu* palm (*Orbignya phalerata*), for example, indicates general fertility. By observing vegetation in a mature forest, experienced colonists can determine the quality of the soils underneath.[29] People who had come to Amazonia long before the highway recognized these differences.[30] Colonists have gleaned knowledge from the *caboclos* who became their neighbors and from their own experience over the last twenty years. As I rode down the side road with Seu Melquiades, he pointed to at least ten different plant species that indicated good or bad soils.

I could not obtain an exhaustive description of soils on each colonist's lot. Nor did I take soil samples to compare with colonist descriptions. However, Emilio Moran did take such samples in the early 1970s and I have compared some colonist descriptions to the empirical data he collected. On a spot-check of three lots, colonist descriptions directly coincided with Moran's findings.

I chose to focus on the colonists' use of soils because it presents the clear-est example of colonist adaptation to the ecosystem. The colonists' ability to recognize soils becomes crucial when they utilize different kinds of soils for different kinds of agriculture, as described in the following chapter.

5

FRONTIER AGRO-ECONOMICS

After the trees in Amazonia, new trees emerge, shorter trees planted in tidy rows, weighted by the fruit of cacao. A farmer walks among them, stopping to examine diseased branches. Several contain tumorous growths; the fruit of those branches rots from the inside. Vassoura de bruxa, *witches broom, has attacked. The farmer pulls the stricken branches as he has done before. No matter how many branches he removes, the disease returns, and worse than before. The price paid for cacao by distributors doesn't compensate for his labor. Soon he will pull up the entire orchard.*

One weekend, Seu Melquiades and I took a trip on his tractor to the end of Side Road 27. Along the way I discovered one of the secrets of his success. We stopped at three different houses to have a cup of coffee, talk about the weather and the presidential elections, and discuss business. Seu Melquiades would always ask how the other farmer's crops were doing. What techniques had he used? Had those been successful or unsuccessful? Why? Observing these conversations, I realized what made Seu Melquiades' farm so diverse, so experimental. On his weekly trips, he would garner farming tips from twenty kilometers worth of side road farmers—how to plant beans to maximize yields, what cultivars to mix within a single field, and how to make degraded pastures productive. He used these tips on his own lot. As one of the oldest members of the community, he sought out the advice of some of his newest neighbors. At fifty-plus years old, he remains an avid student.

Colonists have a lot to learn before they understand the complexities of their ecosystem, and most of them realize it. But time and practice have led them to understand and utilize the land's potential, turning Amazonian biodiversity to their advantage.

Agriculture and Amazonian Land Use

The ecosystem is one of several factors that affect colonists' current cropping patterns—what they choose to plant where. Markets continually influence agricultural decisions. The government's shifting financial and technical support to favor different crops distorts production. Labor and capital requirements have an enormous impact in determining whether a colonist can afford to plant certain crops. The ecosystem presents both obstacles and opportunities for various forms of cropping. I chose to focus on environmental determinants in agricultural decision making, but I will also delineate how these other elements influence cropping patterns on the Transamazon Highway.

This chapter compares different cultivars—annuals, perennials, and pasture—and details two perennial crops in particular, black pepper (*Piper nigrum*) and cacao (*Theobroma cacao*). I compare these in order to demonstrate the effects of soil distribution and labor requirements on cropping patterns. Colonists' decisions to invest in cattle, cacao, or black pepper reflect differences in the quality of soils on their lots and the number of lots a single owner holds.

Different types of agriculture require different types of soils. Cacao survives only in the best soils. Black pepper, another major cultivar in the region, thrives in the worst. Grass grows almost anywhere. After coming to understand their ecosystem, colonists progressed from uniformly planting annual subsistence crops and pasture grass to specializing in crops suited to their lots' soils and terrain. Soils limit colonists' options to diversify their crop base, especially in weak soils. Colonists on weaker soils often rely on cattle instead of crops. On the best soils, colonists are reclaiming pasture lands to put them under crops.

I found that small farmers actually utilize the heterogeneity of their soils, planting black pepper in one spot, grass in another, and bananas and cacao in another, according to what the soils and terrain can support. Small farmers generally plant crops in areas with fertile soils and put infertile areas under pasture. Even in infertile areas, small holder colonists cultivate the few crops that survive in those soils, like black pepper and manioc.

This may seem obvious. Farmers across the globe have always taken soils and terrain into consideration in their agricultural decision making. Amazonian small farmers follow age-old agricultural horse sense. . . . So who cares? One sector of Amazonian farmers does not abide by the obvious.

Medium and large land holders generally do not plant according to the heterogeneity of their soils. They choose to cover even fertile lands with pasture. Large holders must always rely on hired labor, a precious commodity on the frontier. Small farmers employ family labor to farm their lots, perhaps hiring laborers during harvest. Crops demand more labor per unit hectare than cattle. As a result, those farmers who own more than a single 100 hectare lot invariably use what I will call "secondary lots"—lots they do not live on—for cattle ranching, regardless of soil quality. Herein we find a partial answer to the original question of "Why cows?" We can trace deforestation for ranching not only to poor soils, as many researchers have shown, but also to land concentration.

Deforestation for cattle ranching neither increases agricultural production significantly nor provides much employment. With the same amount of land, small farmers feed and employ more people while generating higher returns per hectare. I argue that the decision to promote large landholders was the worst decision the military government could have made—economically and ecologically.

Before comparing small farmers to larger ranchers, we should first examine small farmers' use of the land.

Lavoura Branca: The Annuals

During Emilio Moran's 1973 study, three crops—corn (*Zea mays*), kidney beans (*Phaseolus vulgaris*), and rice (*Oryza sativa*)—dominated the agricultural use of land. They form the mainstay of the typical Brazilian diet. Hoping to feed a burgeoning national population, the government favored these crops by providing credit for them at subsidized interest rates. These crops failed to provide an income for colonists, mostly due to poor government planning. The government did not carefully consider how these crops would be harvested, processed, and transported to the nation's population centers thousands of kilometers away. In the early stages of colonization, the frontier lacked the labor necessary to harvest these seasonal crops, the mechanical equipment to process them, and the infrastructure to transport and store them once harvested.

Settlers who arrived in the early 1970s received land for free or practically free. Those able to work the land staked claims of their own rather than working for others. If farmers were lucky enough to amass the labor needed to harvest a crop, many could not process what they harvested. Rice and beans must be shelled; corn must be husked and have the kernels pulled off. Both must be transported and stored. The highway itself might close for weeks at a time due to downed bridges during the rainy season. Side roads, where most colonists lived and farmed, were closed for months. Many farmers lost their crops due to their inability to pick, store, process, or ship the harvest in time.[1] Though few staples made it out of the Amazon to feed the rest of Brazil, as the government had hoped, local markets were inundated with the only three crops being produced.

The traditional Brazilian agroecosystem, which Brazilians from the Northeast and South knew so well, wouldn't function on the frontier. Farmers from the Northeast, with its chronic underemployment, could scarcely imagine not finding laborers to harvest their crops. Government direction had skewed colonists' decisions and thus skewed markets for labor and products. Colonists counted on a steady demand for their staple crops; they did not foresee an oversupply of food on a frontier where seemingly everything else was scarce. Farmers who borrowed against the projected harvests, betting that strong frontier prices would continue, lost their bets. Some lost their farms.

Colonists learned quickly. Many turned to manioc (*Manihot esculenta*), a tuber native to Amazonia and the traditional staple crop. The government had initially discouraged production of manioc. A modernizing military regime wanted nothing to do with this "backward" crop that fed Indians.[2] The preferential treatment for rice, beans, and corn did not reflect rational ecological or economic analysis, but merely Brasília's urban cultural bigotry.

Manioc offered several advantages over the other staples. Manioc has a protracted harvest, as compared to the few short months during which rice, beans, and corn mature. Farmers leave manioc in the ground until they are ready to process it. No pests or diseases attack manioc on the Transama-

Grating manioc: the whole family joins in grating manioc which has
already been soaked and skinned. Next it will be pressed and cooked.
Wealthier farmers often buy mechanical graters.

zon.[3] The poisonous prussic acid in manioc makes the tuber resistant to
attack. The same acid makes manioc complicated to process in order to
make the tuber edible for humans. But manioc processing demands only
simple technology, not high-cost and high-maintenance threshing machines (*trilhadeiras*). Smith notes a social advantage of manioc that results
from its processing: "Manioc cultivation fosters cooperation and social cohesion, instead of the competition for labor and machines characteristic of
rice farming. Families assist each other in processing flour during the protracted harvest . . . forging reciprocal relationships."[4]

According to Smith, farmers attain higher yields with manioc than with
other annuals—an average of 4,242 tons of processed manioc flour (*farinha*) per hectare as compared to 1,593 kilograms of rice. Manioc produces
three times the number of calories per hectare as rice. The processed flour
stores well for months without spoiling, a distinct advantage in a place
where transportation could be knocked out for months at a time due to
collapsed bridges and washed out roads.[5]

In spite of all its advantages, manioc met an economic fate similar to the other annuals. For a while, the frontier market for manioc collapsed like the others. After avoiding manioc for its low status, farmers started over-producing it when the crops they knew well failed. These four annual crops became known as *lavoura branca*, or "white crops" (implying generic). Due to those initial failures, a stigma remains against beans, corn, rice, and manioc, even though their markets had recovered, and they had become much more lucrative as of 1989 than the crops that replaced them.

Of the four annual crops, only manioc has remained a primary source of income for many farmers. Manioc has held on because it alone of the four can survive and produce in the weak soils covering most of the Amazon. In poor soils or in rocky, mountainous areas, very few other crops will grow—annual or perennial—so the small farmer has difficulty amassing capital with any product other than manioc. The market for manioc has always been limited but fairly stable and provides a steady return.

Today, Transamazonian farmers produce beans, corn, and rice mostly for home consumption and sell their small surplus in town. As a result, this agricultural region is a net importer of staple foods to feed the local urban populations.[6]

Entrepreneurial farmers have recognized the frontier's need for staple crops and are taking advantage of the favorable markets. The Bemvindos mechanized their *terra roxa* lot with a tractor and now cultivate thirty hectares of annual crops alongside twenty-five hectares of the perennial cacao.

Of all his holdings, Seu Melquiades seemed proudest of the little plot of corn, manioc, coffee, and beans in the furthest corner of his lot. This was not the thirty hectares tilled by a tractor for annuals, but his own hand-sown research station on a hectare or two. All his houses, barns, and equipment near the road looked like an accomplishment by any colonist's standard, something to show for twenty years of labor. Mature cacao orchards spread over an entire hill. Nearby, second growth covering thirty hectares suggested the plot's productive history. A bridge he built with his sons spanned the enormous creek running through their lot. He had much to take pride in. But this was it for him, here he beamed. All I saw was leafy ground cover, perhaps laid out in tidy little rows, but filled in between with greenery. To me, it looked a mess. Young beans grew close to the ground. Old stalks of corn poked out of the beans. The stalks had been slashed so that they bent in two, ears drooping until they almost touched the ground. The corn just hung there among the beans, drying and waiting to be picked.

We threaded our way across this field to a thicket of manioc. Other farmers who had shown me manioc had just shown it to me. Seu Melquiades beckoned me to enter the dense growth; he had something for me to see. We ducked and pushed our way inside. After a short distance, I stepped on his prize. Corn grew under the manioc, too. Apparently he used this back plot just to experiment. Would the birds eat as much in here as they did in an open field? Would corn and manioc produce well together? If he cut the manioc down and left the tubers in the ground to rot, would it work well as fertilizer? Surely the native people of Amazonia would know; they have cultivated corn and manioc for thousands of years. Seu Melquiades wanted to learn anew.

The Bemvindos, along with many of their neighbors, experiment with all sorts of cropping patterns to raise yields. They mix several cultivars within the same patch of ground: corn and beans, manioc and corn, beans and rice. Some farmers combine three or four different cultivars within a single field. They time the planting so that no two crops need harvesting simultaneously. This way, during harvest the Bemvindos can rely mostly on the labor of family members (three men and two women) and a second family of workers living on their lot (a couple and their three young children, all under twelve years of age, and all of whom work full time).

Seu Melquiades also mixes annuals with perennials. He showed me a crop of beans planted between rows of one-year-old coffee. In three years, the fully grown coffee would crowd out other plants, but he could harvest one or two crops of beans before then. With the different cultivars utilizing different soil nutrients and maturing for harvest at different times, farmers claim they squeeze more produce out of the same area with less labor expended in preparation and weeding.

Farmers invest significant time in preparing a field (approximately 10 man-days/hectare). If the farmer plants the same area with two different crops, then the area requires less preparation for the second crop. Weeding time (7 man-days for corn) is the same for one or five crops. Farmers reduce the labor investment by double- or triple-cropping an area. By densely cropping an area, they may even crowd out some weed growth.

I spoke with some colonists from the South who prefer to stick with monocultures. They deride this mixed cropping technique as backward, a lazy man's system. One of the newest families from the South disparaged the technique, saying, "People from the South teach the Northerners how to work. Northerners are lazy and disorganized, and they plant confused.

The way they plant, they don't get anything." This southern family has found success thus far with its monoculture of black pepper. Emilio Moran and Nigel Smith noted that such confident southern farmers often changed their ways over time to follow supposedly *caboclo* practices, or even to plant *caboclo* crops, like manioc. Many innovations came about only after colonists met with failure using their traditional methods.

Interestingly enough, the mixed cropping system in its experimental stages begins to imitate cropping patterns found in indigenous swidden plots. The main difference is that colonists' mixed cropping does not initiate the "larger forest management system" of swidden agriculturalists. Once the land stops producing, most colonists abandon the plot completely to second growth or convert it to pasture.

These concerted efforts and experiments with annual crops and mixed cropping appear to be a recent phenomenon. In the 1970s, farmers did not need to worry about maximizing yields from every square inch of ground because they had so much land remaining to put under production. And even if they wanted to maximize production of annuals, local markets for their products were saturated.

Following the early failures of *lavoura branca* annual crops, colonists switched to specialized perennial crop production (*lavoura definitiva*) and to cattle for their primary sources of income.

Specialized Perennial Crops

As colonists became familiar with the local ecosystem and with returns on various cultivars, they specialized. Soon, but gradually, *lavoura definitiva*, the definitive or specialized crops, were introduced. *Definitiva* includes any crop other than the four *branca*. These are almost strictly market-oriented perennial cash crops. After the disaster with annuals, the government switched to promoting certain perennial crops which were well-suited to the Transamazonian environment and which had strong international markets.[7] The government favored cultivation of these crops through bank credits, education programs via agricultural technicians, and assistance in processing. As the migrant labor pool grew on the frontier, as children reached working age, as farmers established themselves financially, and as the government shifted its support, perennials became and remain the preferred agricultural investment.

Cacao and black pepper both enjoyed governmental favor. Each thrives in distinct microecosystems within the Amazon. Cacao requires the best of Amazonian soils, preferably *terra roxa*. Pepper does well in poorer soils (yellow and white sands) but dies young in the nutrient rich soils, after maturing and producing too quickly. When introduced in the mid- to late-1970s, both crops earned high-dollar returns per unit of volume and weight as compared to the annuals. Their price compensated for the high cost of transporting them by road out of the Amazon, as compared to more bulky crops, like bananas. As export crops, they also brought in greatly needed foreign exchange. By giving preferential treatment to some crops, the government distorted farmers' production choices. Cacao and black pepper became ubiquitous on the frontier.

Specialized perennial crops, unlike the annuals, require long-term investments of labor and capital. Table 5.1 shows the annual labor requirements per hectare of various crops and of cattle over the first five years of production.[8] The 22 man-days per hectare for deforestation are figured separately, as they apply to all crops. Most notable is the relatively high labor cost of perennials and low cost of cattle. Preparing the cuttings and the area to be planted, maintaining the plants, then collecting and processing the crop: in all cases, perennials were more complex and time-

Table 5.1. *Labor Requirements for Crops (in Man-Days per Hectare per Year) and Time before First Yield*

Crop	1st Yield	Year 1	Year 2	Year 3	Year 4	Year 5
I. Deforestation		22				
II. Annuals						
Corn	120 days	30	30	30	30	30
Beans	70 days	38	38	38	38	38
Rice	80 days	30	30	30	30	30
Manioc	220 days	*	*	*	*	*
III. Perennials						
Coffee	2–3 years	79	34	30	44	44
Cacao	3 years	251	180	207	171	166
Pepper	2–3 years	232	280	280	280	280
IV. Cattle						
Pasture	3 yr/head	20	6	6	6	6

*Figures unavailable.

Source: Interviews with CEPLAC, EMATER, EMBRAPA, and colonists.

consuming than were the annuals or pasture. Pepper and cacao take two to three years before the first yield and three to five years to clear a profit.

By government calculations, one hectare of black pepper properly cultivated (with government approved inputs of labor, insecticides, and fungicides) requires approximately U.S. $3,000 for the first two years.[9] That's about the cost of buying an entire 100-hectare lot on a side road: a hefty sum of money and labor to invest in one hectare. Few farmers, if any, follow government strictures for planting. Most rely on their neighbors to tell them how to plant, and most distrust the government when it comes to costly fertilizers and chemical applications. Colonists believe the government technicians and bureaucrats get kickbacks from the chemical companies for fertilizer, insecticide, and fungicide sales. Many use fungicides and fertilizers but not necessarily in the amounts recommended by the government. Even without such additions, at 280 man-days per hectare per year, the labor costs remain high throughout the lifetime of the plant. Small farmers find these factors daunting.

Though the initial investment is enormous, so might be the returns. With pepper, the government optimistically projected yields of 4,800 kg/ha in an area with 1,600 plants/ha. At NCr$2.00 per kilogram (approximately U.S.$0.60) in 1989, farmers could pay for start-up costs in one year at full production. Once established, specialized crops can prove highly lucrative. Seu Melquiades Bemvindo and his family grossed approximately U.S.$80,000 in one year on twenty-five hectares of cacao in the early 1980s. Small farmers are not necessarily poor farmers. Prices were high then, and his trees were healthy. With the profits he quickly turned himself into a "medium farmer." He bought two more lots, expanded his cattle herd, and eventually mechanized his primary lot by buying a tractor (on credit) and a thresher.

Some farmers benefited from subsidized credits (low interest and lenient loan standards) if they were willing to take a risk when these crops were first introduced. The risks can be high. In one case the government, in a joint venture with a U.S. investor, introduced *urucú* (*Bixa orellana*, a natural red food dye) in 1985 with plentiful subsidized credits. When the plants began producing, distributors refused to export the crop without a minimum of 100,000 kilos. Amazonian small farmers produced only 50,000 kilos. National consumption could not absorb production and the market crashed. The newest family in the region had invested virtually all their assets in this "hot crop" when they arrived in 1986–1987. The plants stand bedraggled and unattended around their house, but the family leaves them in the ground in case a market miraculously appears. The losses reduced the family to subsistence-level farming. Those who invested in *urucú* were left with worthless investments in perennials and large, low-interest debts.

Subsidies and bank loans became scarce in the late 1980s. Virtually no farmer made a good credit risk after 1988 because land values plummeted and farmers had no other collateral. Many colonists turned over their farms when bills came due. Others simply defaulted. Some indebted colonists were lucky in some ways that their farms were worthless. The banks realized that they could not recuperate their losses by selling a 100-hectare lot with land prices low, so the banks did not foreclose.

The group of sugarcane producers in the CIRA-PACAL cooperative, who will be discussed in following chapters, were an exception to the no-credit rule. Sugarcane requires enormous short-term seasonal outlays of capital. Colonists would cease to produce it without short-term credit for planting and harvesting. The government continues to subsidize cane production, so cane producers continue to find banks willing to lend.

Most of those who were still planting perennials in 1989 obtained the means over time through hard work.[10] I found only one pepper farmer on Side Road 27 who had borrowed money that year to plant perennials, at 20 percent per month from a neighbor. Credit or no, farmers I interviewed reinvested virtually all of their accumulated capital back into the land. Many of them had planted perennials when credit was still available, so I found no shortage of perennial crop farmers on the Transamazon.

A detailed discussion in the next section of two perennials, cacao and pepper, presents the potential benefits and drawbacks of perennial cropping in the Transamazon. Cacao and pepper also illuminate the degree to which Amazonian small farmers have adapted their cropping patterns to their lots' soil qualities. An examination of cropping patterns on different soils will then help answer the question "Why cows here and not over there?"

Cacao: The Rise and Decline of an "Ideal" Crop

Cacao became fashionable early on relative to other specialized crops. Migrants from Brazil's Northeast, where cacao has been cultivated for over a century, already knew this crop well. Unlike other cultivars, cacao had its own bureaucratic supporter in the government's cacao agency CEPLAC

(Executive Planning Commission for Cacao Production), which had vested interests in seeing production expand to other regions of the country. The government had high hopes for cacao in Amazonia, especially in regions with concentrations of fertile soils in which cacao can grow.

Cacao is native to the Amazon and grows wild in the understory. Tree crops hold one distinct advantage over annuals, bush crops (i.e., pepper and coffee), and pasture which is often cited by farmers and agricultural technicians: cacao, banana, palm, Brazil nut, rubber, and fruit trees imitate the forest structure in that they form a canopy when mature. They provide better protection from rain and sun, preventing soil erosion and salt buildup while maintaining moisture and lowering the ground-level temperature. Farmers pay close attention to such environmental changes. They believe their deforestation for pasture and annuals has dramatically altered regional hydrology, lengthening the dry season by several months. As an investment, cacao seemed economically and ecologically sound.

Strains of cacao grown within the Amazon actually have a higher cocoa butter content than those grown in Northeastern Brazil.[11] However, cacao production has succeeded in Brazil's Northeast precisely because the trees were taken out of their native environment. Rainforest species grown as monocultures in their native environment often foster monocultures of voracious native predators—fungi and insects. Smith states that "disease reservoirs exist in close proximity to Transamazon cacao plantations."[12] At the time of his last study in 1979, Smith hypothesized that witches' broom (*Crinipellis perniciosa*) and black pod (*Phytophthora palmivora*) might invade the cacao plantations. That is exactly what has happened. The former, known to colonists as *vassoura de bruxa*, has delivered financial disaster to many farmers. The latter was just beginning to damage crops during my stay.

The *vassoura* fungus requires humidity to grow. Since it is most humid in Rondônia, less so in Pará, and least in the Northeast, Rondônia cacao plantations have the highest incidence and the Northeast the lowest, with Pará falling somewhere in between.[13] *Vassoura* attacks a tree branch by branch, rotting fruit on affected branches from inside. Once it sets in, a farmer must continually pull off affected branches or pull up the entire tree. The government estimates cacao yields ought to begin at 300 kg/ha in the first year and stabilize at 1350 kg/ha in the seventh. These numbers fail to account for the growing incidence of disease in the region. My host family's lot produced 43,000 kg from their mature orchards in 1983 as the govern-

Sunrise at the Bemvindos': standing on a *barcasa*—a platform for sun-drying cacao, coffee, and pepper harvests—a member of the Bemvindo family closes a single sack of dried cacao. The roof on the left rolls over the *barcasa* to protect the product from the rain or night moisture. Before *vassoura de bruxa* (witches' broom) attacked their orchard and lowered production, the Bemvindos dried dozens of sacks of cacao at a time.

ment would have expected; by 1989 production by the same number of trees had dropped below 5,000 kg per year because of *vassoura*. They were lucky. Their trees lived relatively long and productive lives when cacao prices were high and the disease not so pervasive. Trees used to stop producing after about thirteen years. Today they contract *vassoura* as early as two years after planting, resulting in a much shorter productive life span. With increased concentrations of plantations in the region, *vassoura* now spreads more rapidly.

The regional director of CEPLAC in Altamira told me that this single most destructive crop disease in the region was actually curable with enough labor invested in pulling off the affected branches. Everyone else, from farmers to the director's underlings in field offices, had said the opposite; colonists can combat and contain *vassoura* but never cure it. Smith says that as prices rise again, colonists will recuperate their cacao plantings

The harvest: an eight-year-old boy works full time in the cacao groves to earn a
living for his landless family (those with hats in the background).
Here they split open the fruit and pull out the seeds.

by investing enough labor and other inputs.[14] When I asked the director the question again to be certain that "curable" was his answer, he assured me it was. I appealed to the technician standing next to him, who shrugged his shoulders and raised his eyebrows as if to say, "What? You got a problem with that?" The discussion made me realize the extent to which bureaucrats will bend the truth to save their jobs and earn their arm of the bureaucracy more money and influence. If farmers stop planting cacao, CEPLAC loses its reason for existence. So some government technicians continue to say "No problem!" even when prices and productivity levels are falling. Government support—not just for cacao, but for a variety of crops—distorts an already strange follow-the-leader production dynamic. This leaves colonists confused and in a dangerous agroeconomic setting.

Prices paid by distributors no longer compensate for the price of labor necessary to keep the most diseased trees producing. What was the most profitable crop five years ago is a loser today. Colonists have wised up. Few were planting new cacao orchards during my stay, while some were uprooting those orchards already dying.

Black Pepper: Profiting on Poor Soils

Pepper, known by colonists as *pimenta do reino*, followed a trajectory similar to that of cacao. Pepper farmers also face declining yields with increasing incidence of disease over time. The crop was brought to the Transamazon in the 1970s after the traditional growing region of Tomé-Açu near Belém became overrun by disease.[15] As a high-return, low-volume export crop particularly suited to the poor soil conditions found in most of the Amazon, pepper seemed as ideal as cacao—so ideal, in fact, that almost every colonist on Side Road 27 with poor soils has planted it. The government, ever hungry for foreign currency, encouraged the pepper planting frenzy, resulting in overproduction. In 1980, black pepper fetched U.S.$1.20 per kilo, double the current price even without adjusting for inflation.[16] I arrived at the beginning of the pepper season and watched the price drop from U.S.$0.70 to $0.50 per kilo in the span of a month. It was apt to go lower. This drop happens every year during the harvest, when farmers are desperate to sell in order to buy staples or to pay off debts accrued when they had nothing to sell.

As with cacao, disease has struck hard in the young pepper fields. The fungus *Fusarium s. piperi* (called *fusariose* by colonists), which first attacked Transamazonian plantations in the late 1970s, is rampant.[17] If the cuttings are dipped in the fungicide Benlate before planting, the government reports that they stand a better chance of surviving the first two years and that the plants will live longer. Some colonists told me they do not treat cuttings because the fungicide is expensive and they believe the government only recommends Benlate because the government agency garners a profit on sales from the distributor.

Most colonists only recently boarded the pepper bandwagon. Few had planted more than two or three hectares of black pepper by 1989. As the plants take two years to produce and three or four to reach maturity, the price will probably drop further due to overproduction by the time newer plants begin to yield. At the same time, disease will increase their labor costs and lower production per hectare. This is not to say pepper will no longer be profitable, simply that pepper and cacao follow a dangerous path. The price for pepper remains high today and easily compensates for the farmer's initial outlays after two to three years of production (four to five years after the crop is planted). Compared with cattle, pepper provides excellent returns per hectare on poor soils, and colonists know it. Those on poor soils seem to plow as much of their resources and labor into the crop as possible in hopes of escaping the bane of their soils.

I have detailed the history of pepper and cacao in order to point out two tendencies of Amazonian cropping. First, any rainforest crop planted as a monoculture is bound to face increased attacks by disease and pests. Indigenous and forest peoples have adjusted for this historically by planting a variety of species and cultivars, imitating the diversity of the forest. In addition, indigenous and forest peoples clear only small areas, leaving them surrounded by mature forests which act as a buffer against diseases brought in from other plots. Some allow the forest to recover around perennials, thereby providing protection against disease encroachment and pest build up. Colonists have yet to employ these techniques. As the concentration of cacao and pepper plantations has grown in the colonist zone around Altamira region, so have the attacks of fungi and insects.

The government has exacerbated monoculture plantation cropping by favoring certain crops, particularly cacao in the 1970s and early 1980s, and black pepper thereafter. The government is currently experimenting with different cacao varieties and with mixed cropping to protect against disease. A research station near Médicilandia isolated twenty different species of cacao, some of which are resistant to *vassoura*. Others are more productive, and others still respond to different soils and to varying degrees of shade and light.[18] Yet these experiments remain within the basic plantation structure and have not sought to develop more complex systems of forest management. Colonists and the government could learn a lesson from their forest neighbors.

Second, if more and more farmers plant any given crop without significant growth in markets, the price is bound to drop. Cacao and pepper have long established markets, without enormous growth potential. When demand remains stable for agricultural products like pepper and cacao, producers must limit supply if they wish to maintain prices that compensate their efforts. Unless colonists turn to other specialized crops with unexploited market potential, they face highly competitive, even saturated markets for their products.

Even with the perennials' limitations, black pepper, cacao, and other perennial crops remain more productive long-term investments than cattle. Colonists have found crops much more profitable and productive than cattle both per unit area and for return on investment. Small farmers who have the means (labor and capital) and the soils to support crops do plant them.

Cattle Ranching

Analysts have tried to explain the Amazonian cattle phenomenon, attributing it to a stable market for beef, the low capital and labor demands of cattle ranching, tax holidays for cattle ranching, and a desire to clear and maintain as much deforested land as possible for profits on land speculation. Ranching is deeply ingrained in Latin American and Iberian culture. A few colonists told me, *Tudo mundo quer criar gado*, "Everybody wants to raise cows." The myriad of reasons all hold some validity.

Cattle ranching among large holders is easier to explain than among small holder colonists. Well into the 1980s the government provided tax incentives for Amazonian cattle ranching, encouraging deforestation for ventures that would otherwise be unprofitable.[19] These incentives stemmed from the military government's apparent belief that development would follow under the hooves of cattle. They wanted to tame the Amazon.

The tax incentives applied only to large ranchers, not small farmers on 100 hectares.

Large ranchers shared another major concern: fear of expropriation. With presidential elections looming in 1989, many feared that a populist president might freeze money in banks or enact a new land redistribution. For the wealthy, cattle and land serve as investment havens with an unpredictable government and an inflationary economy. Those with capital invested in ranching, not because cattle were necessarily the most productive use of land, but because both land and cattle were fairly liquid investments that would be difficult to expropriate. As stated earlier, once an area is deforested, the rancher gains title to the land and is then protected by the Brazilian constitution. By putting a single cow on a large deforested area, the rancher can claim some notional form of use, regardless of whether the cow uses the entire area. The 1989 election turned out well for landholders. Brazilians elected a fairly conservative president, Fernando Collor de Mello. Collor did freeze bank accounts in February of 1990; he did not redistribute land.

Tax incentives did not apply to or entice small farmers, and they could feel secure that no government would expropriate their 100 hectares. Yet in the early 1970s, even small farmers took their scarce deforested lands out of agricultural production to begin their cattle herds.[20] The pattern became infamous: forest, deforestation, crops, cows.

By my calculations, along with those of Susanna Hecht, Christopher Uhl, and a host of researchers for the Brazilian government, cattle raising is unprofitable or only marginally profitable for the small farmer, without taking land appreciation into account.[21] Edward O. Wilson, author of *The Diversity of Life*, states, "Recent studies indicate that even with a limited knowledge of wild species and only a modest effort, more income can often be extracted from a sustained harvesting of natural forest products than from clear-cutting for timber or agriculture."[22] If a farmer intends to remain on his land, cattle are a marginal investment at best.

So why would a small farmer raise cattle? For small farmers, cattle offer a way to diversify holdings and serve mostly as a bank against disaster. In the case of Ricardo da Souza, he sold forty cows to pay for his operation and for the time he could not work. Unlike crops, which provide cash only during harvest, cattle can be sold quickly at any time. The beasts are also, as Hecht notes, "resistant to the vagaries of tropical ecology."[23] The onslaught of a fungus will uniformly devastate cacao orchards or pepper stands. Of 100 head of cattle on 100 hectares of Amazonian pasture, perhaps one or two, a handful at most, will die each year from eating some noxious weed.

Likewise, local beef markets are resistant to the vagaries of global production and demand. Brazilian cacao competes with cacao from Malaysia and the Ivory Coast. Tropical countries, suffering from debt burdens and unequal terms of trade, compensate for their losses by producing greater and greater quantities of tropical goods, driving down global prices. Whereas prices for cacao, pepper, and other Amazonian exports are determined in commodities markets in Chicago and Los Angeles, beef will be bought and eaten locally.[24]

Most importantly for medium and large holders, cattle do not require the labor or expertise needed to cultivate crops (table 5.1). Rather than improving techniques of tropical farm management (like intensively managing forests), the cattle rancher simplifies. Crop cultivation demands a complex and carefully managed operation; raising cattle is easily done by unskilled workers. A single hectare of pepper requires enormous amounts of skilled labor—280 man-days per year. An equivalent area under pasture would require 6 man-days of unskilled labor per year, or about $\frac{1}{50}$th the work.

Based on differences in labor alone, cattle present a tantalizing alternative for large landowners in a region where land comes cheap and labor dear. Once the plot is cleared for cattle, one hired *gaucho* ("cowboy") can oversee hundreds of hectares of land.[25] Consequently, "Livestock occupied land and created short-term jobs [for deforestation and fencing], but in the end left huge areas cleared of trees and the productive incomes they may have offered in ashes."[26] Cattle ranching strips an area of the possible employment generated by forest extraction or by intensive agriculture, annihilating hopes of sustainable economic development. Small farmers do not have hundreds of hectares; they can scarcely afford to put their land under unproductive pastures.

These low-cost, low-maintenance, low-risk animals provide an equally low but stable return on investment. A fattened cow brings about U.S.$225 after three years. The price fluctuates little. Farmers estimate carrying capacity for cattle to be about one head per hectare, reflecting Smith's and Hecht's estimates.[27] In other words, cattle generate about U.S.$75 per hectare per year and almost no employment. The same hectare planted in black pepper would generate U.S. $3,000 annually and employ one person for most of the year. Compared to black pepper, farmers must deforest forty times the amount of land to generate equivalent economic returns from cattle. Smith holds that when practiced properly, Amazonian cattle ranching can be viable and sustainable for small, medium, and large holders, though small holders will clearly not get rich from ranching.[28] This is not to argue which is more profitable, simply which is more productive per unit area.

The question of productivity and profitability brings an important "externality" into consideration: the environmental costs of deforestation relative to the agricultural returns. Strictly in terms of biomass, the farmer cuts down and burns 395 metric tons (395,434 kilograms) of forest biomass, which support approximately 70 kilograms of animal biomass, in order to plant enough pasture to produce a 300 kilogram cow after three years.[29] Biomass figures ignore the utility of forest products. Often the pasture stops producing after ten years of degradation, compaction, and erosion; then the forest may only partially recover. Colonists have found some creative ways to recover degraded pastures and fields which will be discussed later. Such an abysmal output per unit area of cattle has led researchers to calculate that returns from simple forest extractive industries are higher than the returns on cattle.[30]

Small farmers profit from the labor of family members, which I calculated to be done by hired hands. Small farmers generate their own wages. They gain valuable agricultural skills over time and pass those skills on to their children. By raising crops and employing their agricultural skills, they add value to their product. Hence the fortyfold difference in income generated per unit area of pepper versus cattle. Crop cultivation absorbs their skilled labor with less deforestation.

Small farmers have realized the costs of cattle relative to the returns. Rather than converting their cleared areas into pasture, colonists now employ intensive agriculture where soils permit, attempting to maximize agricultural output on their primary lots with the labor and capital available to them. Some colonists have decided to convert pasture lands back into crops.

Evolving Strategies for Adaptation

One hundred hectares (240 acres) is a large amount of land by almost any farming standard. But as time went on, colonists began to recognize that their 100-hectare lots were limited in what they could produce. Dependent on a single lot for subsistence, small farmers must maximize the output of their lands. To do so, they plant crops whenever possible. Small holders choose cattle as a primary source of income only as last resort, when all else literally fails. Many colonists, especially those on the better soils, now convert areas under pasture back into crops.

Farmers on fertile soils who once planted large pastures now regret it. Pasture grass has become the most tenacious weed in the Amazon. It requires costly and toxic herbicides, long fallow periods, or continued mechanization (tilling with a tractor) to eliminate.[31] *Terra roxa* soils are particularly vulnerable to invasions by a species of grass called *colonião* (*Panicum maximum*) that was introduced from Africa. One *terra roxa* farmer said of *colonião*: *É uma praga, rapaz*, "It's a curse, man, a plague." Escaped pasture grasses provide protection and sustenance to birds and insects which are also agricultural pests.[32] In the fertile sugar growing region, farmers spend huge sums on labor inputs and herbicides to battle the weed. This led at least one EMATER agricultural technician to tell me, *O maior crime desse região é capim e pecuaria*, "The worst crime in this region is grass and cattle."

Colonist Adaptation to a Changing Environment

When trying to reclaim areas from pasture for cropping, farmers are faced with the same environmental and economic conditions that drove them to plant pasture in the first place. The weak markets for agricultural products, lack of capital, and generally infertile soils remain. Add to this degraded and compacted soils, and farmers have a problem. Normally, farmers leave areas to *capoeira*, or secondary forest growth. Natural forest succession breaks up the soils and recharges them with nutrients. Mediocre and poor soils require five to ten years of second growth for even partial recovery. Indigenous swidden systems use much longer periods of second growth, allowing the forest to mature completely.

Small farmers have experimented with means other than second growth to gain higher yields from degraded lands. In areas where the soils have been leached and compacted from exposure and overgrazing, some are planting manioc. The tuber's roots reach deep for nutrients even in the poorest soils. When the plants mature, farmers cut the stems off the manioc and leave the tubers in the ground to rot. The water-swollen roots break up the compacted earth while replenishing topsoil.

They employ similar means to recover worn-out croplands by using what they call *feijão de adubo*, or "fertilizer beans." These they plant between stalks of pepper when the soils have become exhausted. When the beans mature, they are cut and left to mulch, fixing nitrogen in the soils and fertilizing the pepper. In other words, to replenish soils they have exhausted, farmers utilize those same cultivars that are naturally adapted to poor soils. Farmers were forced to use these low-cost inputs because most cannot afford the chemical inputs of modern agriculture. In some ways they are lucky; they have largely avoided the chemical pollution that plagues many agricultural regions of the world, like Central America and California's Central Valley. Low (and appropriate) technology, low capital, and labor-intensive innovations like theirs serve well in a debt-ridden country with high rural unemployment.

Small farmers on the Transamazon have also faced the growing threat of pests over the past few years. They and their government are currently experimenting with alternatives. CEPLAC, for instance, is researching and developing new strains of cacao trees which are resistant to *vassoura*, have a higher fat content, and live longer than the current tree seedlings on the market. Brazil has one comparative advantage over any other country in agricultural research: the largest gene pool on the planet. Commercial products such as cacao, rubber, and quinine all originated in the Amazon. Researchers utilize this advantage to diversify and improve Brazil's agricultural production.

Brazil's gene pool can aid agriculture around the world. Stephen Hubbel and Daniel Janzen learned how to reduce pest damage to crops by observing a traditional pest, the leaf-cutter ant. Leaf-cutter ants bring leaves from forests and farms back to their nests to manufacture fungus for food. To keep their fungi healthy, the ants avoid trees with natural fungicides. By observing which trees the ants avoid, scientists found plant species with natural fungicides.[33] Biologists may breed or genetically engineer natural fungicides into agricultural species. Natural fungicides reduce dependence on chemical inputs and enable organic farmers to compete profitably without damaging the ecosystem. With such discoveries, Amazonia's gene pool may well demonstrate its dollar value in the next wave of technological innovation.

According to Daryl Posey, utilizing biodiversity to their agricultural advantage is one innovation that indigenous peoples discovered long ago. They commonly plant species with natural fungicides in their plots to ward off pests.[34] Colonists have shown their desire to make similar innovations by using manioc and fertilizer beans to resuscitate worn and compacted land and by mixing cultivars to improve yields. Colonists will continue to diversify their crops as some take bolder steps toward forest extraction and management techniques.

Effects of Soil Quality on Agricultural Decision Making

Cropping patterns are surprisingly predictable on the basis of soil quality and distribution. If given a map of soil quality on different lots and whether an individual controls several lots, one could predict fairly accurately what areas would be under pasture, annuals, or perennials, and even determine which perennials would be planted where. Figure 5.1 provides a diagram of fairly typical crop distribution patterns on lots with varying soil types. It should serve as a map for understanding the following section.

Lot 1 diagrams cropping patterns on fertile *terra roxa* soils. Lot 2 shows the typical infertile lot with white sand soils. In general, colonists deforest from the road back to make the cultivated section of their lots accessible. Lot 2 reflects this pattern; crops are in the most recently deforested area in the shadow of the forest. Areas formerly under crops in Lot 2 now lie under pasture or lie fallow as secondary growth. Lot 3 shows a lot with "several" soils, fertile and infertile, with an underlay showing where those soils lie. The fertile soils in Lot 3 line the stream. These soils are probably alluvial, deposited by the stream during high water. Alluvial deposits are often superficial and don't necessarily have the rich substrata typically found under *terra roxa*.[35] The farmer on Lot 3 chooses to plant cacao, beans, and corn in the most fertile soils while putting pasture, pepper, and manioc in infertile areas.

A statistical comparison of crop distribution patterns demonstrates how dramatically soil quality affects agricultural decisions. Both cacao and pepper cultivation strongly reflect soil distribution. Whereas cacao dominates in the most fertile soils, it is rarely found in the least fertile. With pepper, the situation is reversed. Figures 5.2 and 5.3 compare the mean number of hectares under cacao and pepper production on lots of differing soil quality.

Figure 5.3 shows a direct relation between soils and the number of hectares planted in cacao. The more fertile a lot's soil, the greater the number of hectares under cacao production. Pepper follows an opposite trend. Those with white sand cultivate double the amount of pepper of those with

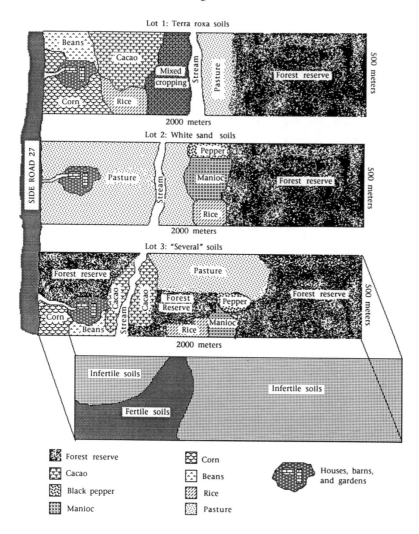

Figure 5.1. Diagram of lots with varying soil fertility.

any other soil; those on *terra roxa* cultivate virtually no pepper since the crop dies young in such fertile soils.

In order to determine whether the differences between these means were significant, I ran an analysis of variance (ANOVA) between the mean number of hectares of cacao planted on the different soil types, as seen in table 5.2.

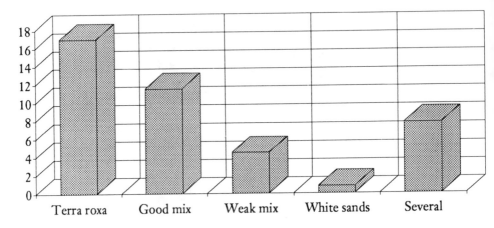

Figure 5.2. Mean hectares of cacao in different soils ($N = 28$).

The Fischer PLSD test indicated a difference in the mean amount of cacao planted on fertile soils and infertile sands at 99 percent (p<.01). In fact, *terra roxa* differed significantly at 99 percent from the categories of weak mix and "several" as well. In other words, the mean number of hectares of cacao on fertile soils differs significantly from the mean number of

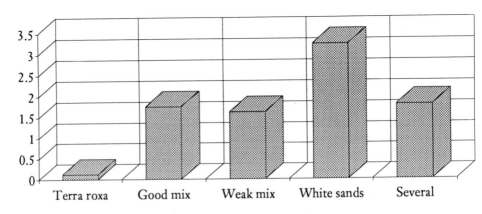

Figure 5.3. Mean hectares of black pepper in different soils ($N = 28$).

Table 5.2. *Comparison of Mean Hectares of Cacao in Different Soil Types (One-Factor ANOVA, N = 28)*

Comparison	Mean Diff.	Fisher PLSD
Terra roxa vs. Weak mix	12.333	11.982*
Terra roxa vs. White sand	16.167	9.66*
Terra roxa vs. "Several"	9.357	9.281*
Good mix vs. Weak mix	6.833	12.278
Good mix vs. White sand	10.667	10.025*

*p<.01.

hectares of cacao on infertile soils at a 1 percent level of error. That good mix did not differ significantly from weak mix (except at the 80 percent level of error) indicates the two soils share relatively similar properties. I found significant differences when comparing black pepper production on different soil types as well. Analysis of variance found differences between the mean number of hectares of black pepper on *terra roxa* and white sand significant at 95 percent (with a 5 percent level of error).

Investments in processing equipment also reflected soil distribution. Farmers on *terra roxa* with large cacao groves built *barcasas*, level platforms on which to dry products such as cacao and coffee. The more expensive *barcasas*, outfitted with rolling roof covers to protect against rains, I found only on lots that had old cacao groves. Farmers with rolling roof *barcasas* probably took advantage of favorable terms of credit in the early 1980s. Owners of white sand lots had their own specialization, the *casa de farinha* where manioc is processed into manioc flour known as *farinha*. All five *casa de farinha* owners I encountered farmed white sand. Survival strategies for both groups relied on taking their cultivars from seedling to finished product to realize maximum returns.

Comparing figures 5.2 and 5.3, one might wonder why the mean number of hectares under pepper production on white sand lots, at 3.25 hectares, stands at about one-fifth the mean number of hectares under cacao production on *terra roxa* lots at 17 hectares. This is due to several factors. First, pepper requires more labor per unit area, so one person can plant less pepper in any given year (table 5.1). Second, some farmers plant their pepper stakes even closer together than the government recommends, one meter apart instead of two, thereby halving the amount of land needed (and per-haps providing more protection for the soils), but significantly raising the labor required. When disease strikes, it will probably spread more rapidly in these concentrated stands. Third, pepper prices did not approach those of cacao in the late 1970s and early 1980s. Colonists could plant more per-ennials back then because subsidized bank loans made capital readily avail-able.[36] By 1989, the price of pepper consistently reached double that of cacao. This led to a shift in planting. More farmers I interviewed were planting new stands of pepper than were planting cacao in 1989. If trends continue, the area planted under pepper may soon match the area planted under cacao. Finally—and perhaps most tellingly—unlike cacao, with its promotional agency CEPLAC, pepper has no equivalent government agency. One agricultural agency, EMATER, gives technical assistance and credit support to all other crops in the region. EMATER's continued exis-tence does not depend so heavily on promoting a single crop.

Pepper's popularity will likely continue because pepper, like manioc, is a survivor. It is one of the only perennial crops able to thrive on infertile soils. Farmers on poor soils have little choice.

What does this mean? Taken together, cacao and black pepper indicate that cropping patterns are predictable on soils of different quality. Clearly, soil quality limits or heavily prioritizes agricultural decision making.

Comparison of Crops to Pasture According to Soil Quality

Like pepper and cacao, the amount of pasture on a given lot reflects that lot's soil quality. Pasture size follows a pattern similar to that of pepper: the amount of pasture grows as the quality of soils decline. Figure 5.4 compares the mean amounts of pasture on lots with different soils.

A lot's area under pasture steadily increases as soil fertility declines. Analysis of variance found lots with white sand to have two and a half times as much pasture as lots with *terra roxa*, significant at 95 percent (p<.05). Farmers on infertile soils appear to invest far more of their land resources in pasture than do farmers on fertile soils.

Farmers who classified their lots as having several soil types break from the patterns in all cases above (figs. 5.2, 5.3, and 5.4). Their combination of soils enables them to plant both pepper and cacao on the same lot. Figure 5.1 diagrams the difference between lots with several soil types and lots containing only white sand or *terra roxa*. The farmer with "several"

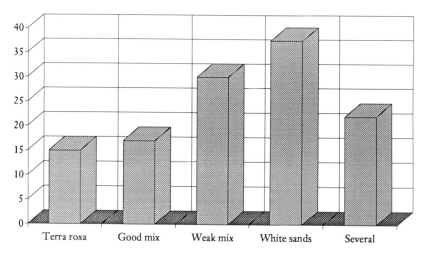

Figure 5.4. Mean hectares of pasture in different soils ($N = 28$).

soils concentrated cacao and annual crops on the most fertile soils. In the area called "Mixed cropping," the farmer might have cacao, bananas, and rubber trees, or coffee, beans, and corn in the same field.

Those with several soil qualities on their lots adapt cropping patterns to have less pasture than those with infertile soils and to have amounts of agriculture comparable to those who have entirely fertile lots. Farmers of "several" soils usually deforested the most fertile areas first and used those for intensive agriculture. Whereas most farmers deforested from the road back, those with "several" soils might deforest three different parts of their lots in order to utilize the most appropriate soils for their cultivars.

One farmer I met, a former truck driver from São Paulo, had a stream toward the back of his lot, surrounded by fertile soils on level terrain. He chose to put his house and the majority of his crops near the stream in order to access the best soils and to use stream water rather than dig a well. His lot met the road on a steep, rocky hill. A sloping path led from the road down to his house, through the forest. The path became precarious at times, twisting around outcroppings of boulders. This colonist considered walking a kilometer from the road to his house and fields better than the alternative. Had he cleared such a steep hill for agriculture, the topsoil would have eroded almost immediately, leaving nothing but scrub and rocks. The lot across the road had neither a stream nor alluvial soils. His neighbor had uniformly rocky, infertile soils on steep slopes. Where his

97

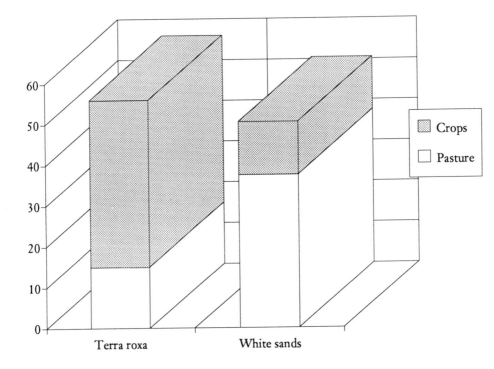

Figure 5.5. Mean hectares of crops and pasture in
fertile vs. infertile soils ($N = 13$).

neighbor had deforested the hill near the road, exposed rock and sand made
it look like a wasteland.

For these farmers, terrain also limits agricultural decisions. The Amazon
is full of hilly and rocky areas. When deforested, steep slopes erode much
more rapidly than flat areas, as I saw that day while hitching a ride out of
Médicilandia. Extremely rocky areas are difficult to farm, as rocks obstruct
tilling and planting and reduce the area available for agriculture. If they
have options, colonists leave areas with steep slopes or rocks for forest
reserves.

The combination of weak soils and poor terrain can ruin attempts at cropping. Figure 5.5 provides evidence to the disparities between lots with fertile and infertile soils. It compares the mean number of hectares under all crops to the mean number of hectares under pasture for the most and least fertile soils.[37]

Farmers on infertile white sand plant small areas with what few crops they can, leaving the remaining agricultural land under pasture; those on fertile *terra roxa* rely least on pasture, utilizing most of their agricultural land for cropping.

Farmers on white sand crop a mean of just under fifteen hectares (mostly pepper, manioc, and rice), while their pastures are enormous, a mean of thirty-seven and a half hectares. Once white sand is used for more than two or three years for all but pepper and manioc, it must either be left fallow as

The fate of white sand farmers: one hectare of new pepper stakes,
ninety-nine hectares of grass and scrub, and no mature forest cover this lot.
The forest lies two and a half kilometers back from the road.

secondary forest growth or be converted to pasture. Even pepper needs some fertilization after about five or six years in order to survive in these soils. In contrast, farmers on *terra roxa* cultivate a mean of over forty hectares, with fifteen mean hectares of pasture. Farmers on fertile soils can plant beans and corn year after year, along with a variety of other cultivars such as coffee and sugarcane that will not grow on infertile soils. The cattle which *terra roxa* small farmers keep produce meat and milk mostly for family consumption. *Terra roxa* small farmers continue to maintain so much land under pasture partly because of the difficulties they encounter in reclaiming pasture lands for agriculture.

Implications for Long-Term Trends in Amazonian Cropping Patterns

A pattern emerges to account for the preponderance of pasture and ranching on the agricultural frontier. Infertile areas—80 to 90 percent of Amazonian *terra firme*—will be converted from verdant rainforest to marginally productive pasture.

While cropping patterns follow soil quality, prices follow supply and demand. Cacao production is naturally limited by the area in which it will grow, since 7 percent or less of the Amazon is covered in the *terra roxa* soil cacao needs. Much of the *terra roxa* lies in the more humid regions of Acre and Rondônia less suited to cacao growth. In addition, those who own fertile soils can rely on other crops as a source of income when global cacao prices are low. *Terra roxa* farmers may feel secure that their options will remain open and profitable.

Black pepper farmers cannot feel so secure. Literally millions of square kilometers of acidic infertile sands remain in Brazil under mature rainforests. If Brazilians open this land to colonization and deforestation, the result will be painfully predictable. Infertile sands limit what colonists can produce. This land may support varied cropping immediately after mature forests are burned, but within two to three years, only manioc, pasture, and pepper will survive among the array of cash crops currently planted in Amazonia. Farmers on infertile soils do not enjoy the luxury of choice. Whereas cacao producers can and do diversify to avoid overproduction, black pepper producers cannot.

Colonists with infertile soils face steadily declining prices for their few crops when more infertile areas are deforested and put under production.

As prices fall for their crops, the sandmen of Amazonia (farmers like Sandman on infertile soils) will turn to cattle as their primary source of income. Consequently, small farmers themselves have suggested that infertile areas be left as forest reserve and that only the more fertile regions be distributed for small holder colonization.

If only the fertile lands were opened to single lot, small farmer colonization, my findings predict that cattle would no longer predominate on frontier farms. But most of the zone expropriated in 1970 by the PIN program has not been occupied by single lot small farmers. Some *terra roxa* lots lie entirely under pasture. To account for the difference, one must look not to environmental woes of acidic infertile soils, but to socioeconomic woes—to the uneven distribution of land.

When farmers expand their holdings from a single lot (referred to here as primary lots), they consistently devote their second and third lots (secondary lots) to pasture. The above analysis considered only primary lots, or "small" farms. Below, agricultural patterns among "medium" holders will be examined.

Patterns of Cropping and Pasture According to Land Distribution

Much has been made of the differences between Amazonian colonists and owners of *glebas* (known as *glebistas*).[38] Large holders account for most of the cattle ranching while creating little employment or few agricultural products. Even among colonist small farmers in the Amazon, land is not evenly distributed . . . nor are the agricultural products evenly produced. Moran took pains in his study to show that colonists were not some "undifferentiated peasantry" exploited by external capitalism: "In fact, some of these same farmers became not just tools of capitalism, but capitalists themselves."[39] Though INCRA prohibited anyone from owning more than one lot in the colonist zone, a land market quickly grew up there, and some successful colonists began amassing several lots while the government turned a blind eye.

Medium and large holders broke away early from the pattern of cropping seen among small farmers. In 1973–1974, Moran recognized the "entrepreneurial" farmer's propensity to expand landholdings and put areas under pasture rather than cropping.[40] Some colonists moved off the land into the city, hiring unskilled laborers to oversee their herds. Thus the classes

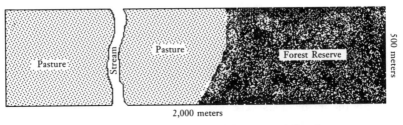

Figure 5.6. Diagram of typical secondary lots of all soil types.

of absentee landholders and landless workers developed in a colonist zone created in the name of social justice and equality, for the express purpose of creating a yeomanry.

Since I surveyed only those owners who lived on the land, the "absentee" landholders in my sample actually live and farm primary lots in the area while overseeing their secondary lots. Like their city-going brethren, the medium holders I interviewed used their secondary lots for cattle ranching. Figure 5.6 diagrams cropping patterns on the typical secondary lot of a single owner.

Colonists buy secondary lots for various reasons—to diversify holdings, to speculate on land values, to protect against inflation, and to expand the grazing area for their growing cattle herds. Whatever their reasons, the result is always the same. Virtually all land cleared on secondary lots is put under pasture, as demonstrated in figure 5.7, comparing the mean amounts of crops and pasture on primary and secondary lots. On the primary lots of all colonists in my sample, the mean amounts of cropping and pasture were roughly equal, with 21.4 hectares of crops and 23.1 hectares of pasture (an approximate 1:1 ratio). In contrast, secondary lots had a mean of 46.8 hectares of pasture and 2.6 hectares of crops (an approximate 20:1 ratio). Secondary lots compare poorly even with the sample of infertile white sand with its 4:1 pasture to crop ratio. Analysis of variance found the 23.68 hectare mean difference between pasture on secondary and primary lots to be significant at the 99 percent level, even without taking the soil quality of the first lot into consideration.

Soil quality does not account for the use of pasture on secondary lots. Secondary lots had an even distribution of soil quality, as is shown in the breakdown in figure 5.8, which presents the soil qualities encountered on secondary lots in my sample. Interestingly enough, not one owner designated a secondary lot as having several soil types. Some of them had labeled their primary lots as having several types of soil and farmed accordingly. On their secondary lots, however, farmers did not differentiate. Whether or not soils on different parts of the secondary lot were fertile mattered little to them. Be it the second, third, or fifth lot of a single owner, *terra roxa* or white sand, secondary lots were used uniformly for pasture. Most had no agriculture whatsoever, as shown above in figure 5.6.[41] In the one case in which a colonist bought a second lot that had better soil quality than his primary lot, he and his family moved to the lot with better soils to farm it as their primary lot. They left one son to oversee the herd and weed out second growth on their old lot.

My sample of secondary lot owners contains only those who might be considered "medium holders" by colonist standards (500 hectares or less), with one exception (a man who controlled six lots). Although large holders did not fall under the purview of my study, colonists reported that the *glebas* of 500 to 3,000 hectares at the end of their side roads were entirely under

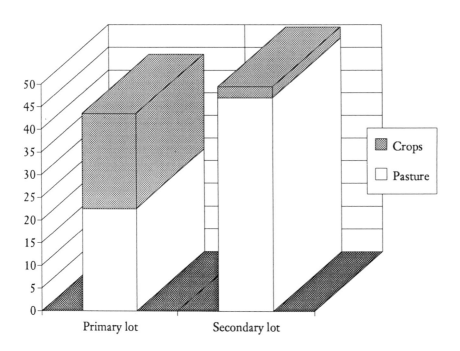

Figure 5.7. Mean hectares of pasture and crops on primary ($N = 28$) vs. secondary ($N = 11$) lots.

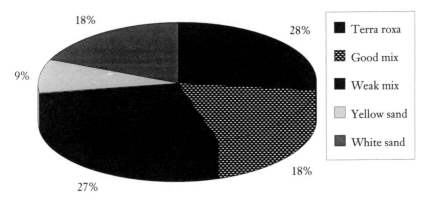

Figure 5.8. Soil types in secondary lots (*N* = 11).

pasture, if they were cleared at all. I did speak to one former *glebista*. He was unique in that his *gleba* was close to the highway and therefore had access to a pool of day laborers. Nevertheless, he told me he had fewer than fifty hectares of crops on those 3,000 hectares. Much of the rest he deforested for ranching.

The axiom which Bill Durham observed in El Salvador holds true in the Brazilian Amazon: "Land is scarce only for the small holders."[42] Medium or large holders needn't maximize production in order to maximize profits. They do not profit from working family members. They must hire people at frontier wages to cultivate their lands. For medium and large holders, the labor costs of cropping are prohibitive; the incentives to raise cattle become overwhelming. With cattle, a large holder can oversee several lots alone or employ a single hired hand. Therefore, large holders opt to raise cattle.

Lessons from Another Frontier

Ever since my arrival in the Amazon, I had asked myself why cows had become ubiquitous across the globe and if we could find a more appropriate use than cattle for land. I encountered an expert with some answers to my questions on an altogether different frontier.

In the summer of 1992, I finally made it to Alaska for a season of backpacking. Toward the end of my stay, five guys from California met me in

Fairbanks. Together we took a small plane to the Brooks Range, about a hundred miles north of the Arctic Circle. We put in with three canoes at the headwaters of the Noatak River. In two and a half weeks and 300 miles of paddling, we saw only four other human beings. Few things in this world can compare to that wilderness.

The oldest and wisest paddler was Dr. Bradford P. Smith, Professor of Veterinary Medicine at the University of California at Davis. While the others fished, Brad and I often spent our mornings hiking around the Brooks Range, taking pictures, and chatting about this and that.

Brad knew all about cows, having spent half his life rearranging their intestines as a professor of surgery and large animal internal medicine. Living in Davis, he hangs out with a rancher or two. On one of our walks, while looking up a ridge where Dall sheep chose their precarious path and looking out over oxbow lakes dotted with grazing moose, Brad ventured, "Ruminants are the wave of the future."

Well, that's great, Brad, I thought, just what we need. More grass, more cows, more methane flatulence. No, he explained, the way we've gone about raising ruminants is all wrong. We should *ex*tensify rather than *in*tensify. Grazers need space, like these moose and sheep up here, he said. Ranches in the U.S. don't run that way. They plant nonnative grasses that maximize yields but leach the soils; they spray with herbicides and pesticides to keep the grass "healthy" and the weeds out; then they stuff too many cows into a fenced area, until the soil is so compacted and depleted that the only plants that will grow are thistles and weeds. The solution? Ranchers respond to overgrazing with more herbicides and pesticides and throw in some fertilizer. The longer they do so, the more chemical inputs they need to maintain production. Eventually, the land becomes so worn-out that the chemicals don't work. That's no solution, said Brad.

Brad said native grasses would do just fine. They did just fine for the millions of years when California had natural grasslands that produced millions of tule elk. Do you realize, Brad queried, that tule elk used to roam the entire Central Valley of California? Now only a few small herds of these elegant and tasty ruminants remain. Cattle ranches, water projects, and crops crowded the tule elk out of their native habitat.

With native grasses, and perhaps native ruminants, we wouldn't need any herbicides to keep out "weeds." The weeds we'd need to battle would be the European grasses now in use which exhaust the land. It's a pretty simple idea: return to raising ruminant species native to the regions in which they evolved and resuscitate their native habitats.

Inuit people of Alaska hunt the caribou we saw in the Brooks Range. Laplanders herd reindeer. I have heard of iguana growers in Central America who are trying to revive one of their traditional sources of protein. But tule elk herders in California? What a concept. Why not? If we want meat, bring back the tule elk, let the buffalo roam, let the prairie become prairie again. Reseed it if need be.

What does all this have to do with Amazonia? Well, when Brad first said ruminants were the wave of the future, this Amazonian researcher thought that meant replacing more forests with grasslands. Now I see that's not at all what he meant. Ruminants have always made agriculturally marginal lands productive; hence, people have historically herded sheep in deserts and reindeer in the Arctic. Forests, by contrast, can produce plenty for human use and consumption. Brad thinks ruminants ought to ruminate on the hills and plains with native grasslands, not those covered in rainforests. Let ruminants eat where people can't.[43] Cutting down an American rainforest to plant African grasses and introduce European ruminants for profit is nuts, according to Brad's way of thinking. Mine too.

The question "Why cows?" in the Amazon was posed in the first chapter of this book. A preponderance of cattle on the frontier stems from Amazonian land distribution policies and the quality of the land distributed. Although marginally productive economically and disastrous ecologically, cattle seem a reasonable adaptation to a market economy for the small farmer on infertile soils. These farmers can plant little else; they do not understand the forest well enough to employ forest management; and they would have difficulty finding markets for forest products even if they did engage in extractive industries. Cattle are reasonable for the large holder who has abundant lands where labor is scarce. If Brazilians want to avoid replacing rainforests with cattle ranches, Brazil must reexamine its land distribution policies.

CONSIDERING A SECOND RE- DISTRIBUTION

After the trees in Amazonia, a researcher waits for a ride on the Transamazon Highway. Dust, the omen of approaching truck. Dust, rumble, cab, cargo, tail, tail, tail, tail, tail, head, tail, tail. Looks like old Bessy got turned around. Situation doesn't make much sense to Bessy. Cows in the Amazon. Doesn't make much sense to the researcher either.

Considering the radical disparities of wealth in Brazilian society, the outsider has difficulty understanding why social pressures have not already forced a land redistribution. A strong case can be made for agricultural land reform and an equitable income distribution in Brazil's South and Northeast. Without such reform, Brazilians will spontaneously colonize and farm the Amazon.

If colonization proceeds, it ought to take the environment into account alongside economic considerations. My research adds to the large body of literature which indicates that the opposite has taken place. Colonists suggest that alternatives to the destructive pattern are available. Economically, small farmers are more productive than medium or large farmers per unit hectare. They employ skilled labor and utilize more of the land's potential once it is deforested. They even produce export crops, much to the debt-strapped government's pleasure. This could hardly be said for corporate ranchers. Yet small farmers' demands have been consistently ignored while 80 percent of the area expropriated by PIN has been designated for huge ranches.[1] The questions are, who should do the colonizing and which part should they colonize?

Based on interviews with colonists concerning what they think is equitable and possible and based on the agricultural patterns indicated by the data I collected, I would suggest a three-part program:

I. Protection of Primary Forests: Forested areas ought to be protected and controlled by their original protectors, the forest peoples.

II. Redistribution: Large cattle ranches with fertile soils that have been deforested ought to be given to small farmers.

III. Reforestation of Infertile Areas: Infertile areas already deforested for ranching ought to be reforested by "forest managers."

I. Protection of Primary Forests

What is left of the forest ought to be set aside as "extractive reserves" for forest peoples. Colonists would argue against this. Forested areas have been depopulated by disease and rural-urban migration, leaving a few hundred thousand occupants where millions once lived. Many colonists resent Native Americans and forest peoples for claiming such large tracts of Brazil, when many Brazilians have nothing. On their part, native peoples would point to a 500-year decimation of their populations and traditional land holdings. Colonists have encroached far enough, many would say. Colonists and native peoples will have difficulty coming to terms over questions of land equity and rights.

I suggest that forest peoples gain legal control of the forests out of environmental rather than social concerns. Unlike the colonized zone, areas which forest peoples now control remain mostly under forests. Forest peoples understand the forests better than anyone else, have proven the sustainability of their subsistence and extractive systems, and ought to be given title to the areas they use. Forest families or communities would control large areas of forest, using most of it for extraction while cutting small plots for subsistence agriculture.

The government of Fernando Collor de Mello recently set aside extractive reserves in rubber tapping areas and granted large areas to native tribes, such as the Yanomamö. The reserves provide families with far more than the 100-hectare lots typical on the Transamazon under the assumption that extractive industries require larger areas in comparison to agriculture in order to be profitable. Now rubber tappers on these reserves enjoy government protection against encroachment by ranchers or colonists and have incentive to care for the forests. These first extractive reserves may serve as testing grounds for more extensive ones.

Nigel Smith reports that some extractive reservists have begun small-scale ranching.[2] Ranching violates the spirit and principle of the reserves. If treated as normal land holdings, extractive reserves would fall under the designation in this book of large holdings or *glebas*. Some penalty must be set to prevent extractive reserves from following the path of large farms in Amazonia. The government might even revoke extractive reserve status for severe violations. I would not suggest penalizing reservists for raising a small number of cows for family consumption. Small plots of grass can exist within a swidden system of rotation and forest resuscitation.

Some forest peoples already drive larger herds of a kind. A member of the Runa tribe of Ecuador told anthropologist Dominique Irvine, "The animals of the forest are our cattle. We care for them."[3]

II. Redistribution

Where cattle ranches have already encroached, the forest peoples are mostly gone, as are the forests. Ranchers have done their damage, often having forcibly evicted former forest inhabitants before deforesting. In these areas, I propose letting small farmers have a chance to do what they do best: make deforested areas productive.

Rather than allowing continued distribution of mature upland primary forests, the government ought to enact a second redistribution on land that has already been deforested, one that actually favors small farmers, as was promised the first time. Since even medium holders fall into a pattern of using fertile lands for cattle ranching, farm sizes in the Amazon should be restricted to areas that families can cultivate sustainably with the labor of family members. The question of sustainability would have to be addressed for an intensive agricultural system in which fallows are integral to maintaining productivity. Phillip Fearnside has done extensive research on carrying capacity along the Transamazon since the early 1970s. My own observations indicate that a lot of 100 hectares of fertile soil requires more than enough labor for any single family to cultivate, even if that lot is highly mechanized. On the most fertile soils, where fallows are not as crucial, the area should probably be smaller.

A wide range of literature on colonization in Latin America as well as the colonists themselves suggests that redistribution should be done spontaneously, with as little governmental bureaucratic interference as possible. Moran, Foweraker, Nelson, and others argue that spontaneous colonization is relatively inexpensive and effective in building a community because settlers choose the best agricultural lands.[4] Spontaneous colonization sharply contrasts with the government-directed colonization that took place in the early 1970s in which the quality of the land was scarcely considered.[5] When the landless occupy ranchlands that are fertile, the government could protect them against any *glebista* ranchers who use violence to guard land that they claim.

If current laws were enforced in the colonized zone, colonists would be restricted to owning no more than a single 100-hectare lot. If such laws were extended to the zones of huge *glebas* (ranches of 500 hectares or more), ranchers would have no incentive to deforest, knowing that their lands would be expropriated, regardless of alleged improvements. Those colonists currently vying for land could occupy the more fertile areas that have already been deforested by *glebistas*.

Not all areas are suitable for intensive agricultural or agroforestry settlement, so not all deforested areas should be redistributed to colonists. Brazilian policy makers might look to the lessons of past Amazonian cultures to find which areas are most appropriate for agriculture. Remnants of past cultures may be found under mature second growth forests, the *mata de cipó*.

Balée argues that the most fertile black earth Amazonian soils, found beneath these forests, resulted from indigenous peoples' soil management.[6] My study suggests that the fertility of anthropogenic soils was probably more a cause of occupation than a result of it. Colonists with "several" soils on their lots look for the *mata de cipó* as a sign of good soil quality and deforest those areas first. Native peoples probably chose to farm those areas for their fertile soils in the first place. This is not to discount Balée's argument that native peoples may have improved the quality of the soil, but to suggest that indigenous peoples probably occupied those areas precisely because the soils and terrain were the most fertile and most hospitable to agriculture. Their occupation over thousands of years altered the ecosystem by lowering species diversity while maintaining protein production.[7]

Indigenous peoples' alterations of the ecosystem serve as signposts to modern Brazilians. Small farmers ought to occupy and make productive fertile areas where large holders have cut down liana forests for ranching.

I should clarify that I do not advocate decimating the liana forests. They, too, should be valued as a unique ecosystem, even if they are less diverse than primary forests. Large concentrations of *terra roxa* once covered by *mata de cipó* have already been converted to agricultural production, while much of the rest is heavily used for extractive industries. One concentration of *terra roxa* lies in Rondônia, where the heaviest colonization has taken place, and much of the forest is gone. A concentration in Acre, adjacent to Rondônia, also contains the highest concentration of natural rubber trees in Brazil. Rubber tapping remains a viable industry there; tappers have fought bitterly to protect the forest from ranching encroachment. The stretch of *terra roxa* near Altamira which stretches across Side Road 27 and surrounds Médicilandia represents some of the finest arable land in Amazonia. Other than those, areas of *terra roxa* are relatively small and rare. The government should not build a highway to every pocket of fertile soil in Amazonia. If policy makers do allow continued deforestation or even experiments in forest management, the *mata de cipó* areas may offer the best soils with the lowest impact on species diversity apparently because diversity in these forests has already been reduced by indigenous settlement.

III. Reforestation of Infertile Areas

Finally, areas with infertile soils are inappropriate for most forms of intensive agriculture and ought to be returned to forest cover. Black pepper and manioc sustain some farmers now, but markets for both products are limited. The recent decline in the price of pepper indicates some market saturation. Brazil should restrict access to its abundant infertile lands, thereby limiting the production of cultivars which survive on those lands and avoiding market collapse.

Infertile areas that have already been deforested by ranchers should therefore be targeted for reforestation projects. Several means of financing such ventures internationally have been implemented recently in Brazil and elsewhere. Both debt reduction for reforestation and reforestation financed by industrial companies in order to offset carbon emissions look promising.

These programs may offend some sensibilities by threatening national sovereignty. Those who object might turn to national lumber companies that have a long-term interest in developing sustainable forestry.[8] In December of 1990, Brazil approved its first major Amazonian reforestation plan, with a price tag of $3 billion. The plan proposes to reforest 2.5 million acres (approximately 1 million hectares) in an area deforested for ranching and charcoal production for the Grande Carajás iron ore project. It will be financed not only by foreign capital, but also by the Brazilian industries that contributed to the deforestation. The company mining the iron ore, Companhia Vale do Rio Doce, made the proposal.[9]

Moran informed me that some colonists of the Transamazon have also entered the business of reforestation. In his 1992 survey of second growth on the Transamazon Highway, Moran found one colonist who planted mahogany seedlings for his second growth. At close to $700 per cubic meter of wood, that colonist's children will profit handsomely from his foresight.[10] On his farm, we see the beginnings of colonist management of second growth. Reforestation could prove positively lucrative, providing jobs and relieving the outflow of foreign reserves.

Implementing Land Reform

Implementing land reform would be a complicated and difficult undertaking. Even if the government passed new laws which stated that no individual could own more than, say, 100 hectares of deforested land, the laws would be difficult to enforce and probably lead to serious and violent conflicts over the land.

Rather than forbid large holdings, the government could simply discourage them through a land tax. Much of the deforestation resulted from tax breaks for cattle ranches. Tax hikes may be just the tool to reverse the damage. Cattle ranchers deforest in order to gain title to land, as described in the introduction. Once they have a title, they profit by selling deforested land. Rather than handing a title to people who deforest large areas, the government should hand them a bill. A tax could be applied to any deforested parcel larger than 100 hectares being sold. If the land tax were progressive, then the larger the area deforested, the larger the bill for a land title. Thus, deforestation would become less and less desirable for economically unproductive activities such as cattle ranching and land speculation. This tax would reverse the age-old tradition in Iberian cultures of favoring large land holders and cattle.

Large holders would attempt to find ways around a land tax. INCRA had prohibited colonists from owning more than one lot in certain areas of the colonization zone (mostly along the highway). In these areas, the government stipulated that only males over twenty-one years of age could own lots. Except for its gender bias, this prohibition would have been a good law had it been enforced. It was not, however, and colonists often own two or more secondary lots (hence the designation here of secondary lots). Colonists and large holders found loopholes to evade the prohibition: they placed lots in the names of each of their children or in the names of fictitious family members. Eventually INCRA and its successor MIRAD seemed to accept some individual colonists' de facto ownership of several lots.

At present, small holders are just as likely to deforest their properties as large holders. Small holders may make cleared lands more productive than large holders, but they still clear the land. Small holders deforest fewer hectares than large holders only because they have smaller properties to deforest. When colonists become medium holders, they plant pasture grass on secondary lots just like large holders. If *all* large holders' lands were redistributed to small holders, deforestation would probably continue. That's why I suggest redistribution only of already deforested lands. Implicit in my argument is a belief that primary forests are more valuable to humanity, to the earth, and to Brazil than second growth forests or agriculture.

The situation could be improved, first, by enforcing the single lot law as it stands and, second, by requiring owners to reside on the lot to which they claim title. Owner residency would provide some guarantee that a lot is not one of many overseen by a single *vaqueiro*, or cowboy. The distinction between primary and secondary lots made earlier reflects actual land use patterns on the frontier: colonists crop the lots on which they live, and they plant grass and herd cattle on their other lots. From an ecological standpoint, medium holder colonists are no better than large holder cattle ranchers in regard to their secondary lots. Requiring owners to reside on their lots provides no guarantee that owners will use the lots efficiently. These government-imposed restrictions would merely encourage efficient use as well as limit the environmental damage one owner could inflict.

Again, restrictions could be enforced through taxation. If owners could not prove they lived on the lot to which they claimed title, they should be taxed an amount of money large enough to make absentee ownership prohibitive. If an owner tried to avoid the law by claiming a lot through deforestation but not claiming title to it, then landless people and aspiring small farmer colonists should have the opportunity to occupy and claim the land in question.

The government's primary responsibility in the redistribution program would be to withhold titles to deforested lands from large holders or to grant them at great annual cost. As a teacher working with sixth graders during the last year, I've come to realize that one can provide incentives and encouragement until the cows come home and still have to lay down consequences for bad behavior. Such is life.

Small farmers and the landless would have to carry out the actual redistribution of land themselves. They would need to act collectively in their own interests against the interests of large ranchers through a vigorous program of land occupations sanctioned by law. This would, of course, require a great deal of cohesion and organization among small farmers. The development of small farmer grassroots organizations forms the subject of the following chapter. I argue that small farmers are in the process of building the grassroots organizations necessary for a second land reform.

7

THE RISE OF COLLECTIVE ACTION

After the trees in Amazonia,
after the government in Amazonia,
colonists remain. One holds a baby in
her arms as the infant shakes from
fever. She doesn't know if her baby
can survive the 18 kilometer trip out
of the side road to the health post for
treatment. Another colonist walks
from house to house to organize his
neighbors. He wants a health post
on the side road for the time his
babies become ill.

The current Brazilian government would likely give one simple response to an ambitious proposal for land redistribution: *Não têm condições.* Even if bureaucrats in Brasília had the will to enact a land redistribution, they don't have the means. If colonists want a just and rational distribution of land on the frontier, they will have to carry it out themselves.

Since 1980, Amazonian colonists have shown themselves capable of enacting a redistribution as they have organized and acted collectively to achieve several difficult communal goals. This chapter traces the rise of collective action and democratic systems of local government during the withdrawal of a paternalistic, authoritarian regime.

I first encountered the fruits of collective action on my walk down Side Road 27. Fallen and rebuilt bridges were hard to miss; every three kilometers or so I would pass another one. Though Eduardo, the truck driver, had told me most side roads were impassable after a few kilometers due to downed bridges and forest invasion, this road and all its bridges seemed to

Figure 7.1. Poster from the Rural Workers' Union of Uruará.
The text reads, "Without organizing your thoughts, force is useless. You must
organize your thoughts, and join forces."

be in decent shape (except for the large erosion/drainage pit running down
the side of it). Why was Side Road 27 so different from the others? While
colonists on other roads waited for the government to come fix bridges and
repair the road, colonists on Side Road 27 held *reuniões*, "get-togethers,"
and did the repairs themselves.

Researchers on the Transamazon in the 1970s often wrote of the difficulties that colonists had in organizing for collective action and in forming cooperatives on the frontier. Well into the 1980s, researchers hypothesized that cooperativism would not take hold on the frontier in the near future.[1] Few neighbors stayed long enough to get to know each other, let alone trust each other. Ninety percent or more of the colonists moved on within the first ten years of settlement. Due to the precipitous rate of onward migration, colonists had difficulty in building a community and working toward communal ends. More often, they turned for help to a paternalistic government, organized as a military bureaucracy to direct change from the top down. Colonists' needs were met slowly and inefficiently, if at all. But the government ran out of paternalism when it ran out of money. After 1980, fallen bridges remained fallen for years.

Some colonist communities filled the political vacuum with their own organizations. Whereas Moran and Smith actually witnessed cooperatives and communal associations on the decline in the 1970s, these nascent organizations now dominate the political culture of the region. I devoted a significant portion of my study to the rise of local initiative—on Side Road 27, at the CIRA-PACAL sugar refining project, and in other areas of the highway—focusing on what forms of collective action the colonists have developed to address their continuing needs. I argue that rural development and even land redistribution on the frontier can be achieved most effectively, not through government direction, but through local initiative and grassroots collective action. The government would not disappear in this scheme. It would remain as an arbiter of competing interests and protector of the nation's environment and resources.

Individually, very few members of the community have the *condições*, the means to overcome the impediments that colonists face on the frontier. Collectively, they have improved prices, bridges, roads, and even education and health services. I asked colonists how that collective action came about, where it is now occurring, and why. The question of why was partially answered during my conversation with Eduardo, before I ever saw Side Road 27. Colonists form grassroots organizations out of necessity.

The Associations

Eduardo and I had been talking about the military government's failed promises—schools, health posts, open side roads, paved highways. The list seemed endless. As we bounced along, somewhere between Marabá and Altamira, I asked Eduardo, "Do you want the highway paved?" almost certain I knew the answer. His spine would be wrecked soon enough by the truck's pounding. To my surprise, he gave an emphatic *Não*. If it were paved, he explained, his company would have more competition. As it is, he and his company make a killing, even though it takes five days to drive one direction on the Altamira-Cuiabá route in the dry season and four weeks during the rains. Prices are high on the frontier; difficulties in transportation are one reason for that.

For frontier farmers, Eduardo and his company's fortunes spell disaster. Though six different distributors buy the colonists' goods, one, DISPAM, controls 90 percent of the market. DISPAM sells cacao to the multinational Nestlé Corporation in São Paulo. Numerous farmers and truck drivers, along with government officials, reported that the distributors formed a cartel which met weekly to agree on prices—far below national prices—at which they would buy farm products. For instance, the price for Transamazonian cacao while I was there hovered between U.S.$0.25 and $0.35 per kilogram, while the same kilo of cacao would fetch twice or even three times that price in the Northeast, the traditional cacao growing region of Brazil. Worse yet, the Amazonian price is one-sixth of the price that Amazonian farmers received for cacao in 1979 when it sold for U.S.$2.00 per kilogram.

Over the last ten years, the global price of cacao has dropped precipitously because worldwide production has increased while demand has remained relatively stable. In the 1970s, Brazil entered an international accord to limit production and maintain a high price for cacao, forming a cartel modeled after OPEC. But the Ivory Coast, the largest producer, violated that accord by making special pacts with the United States.[2] In return, Brazil increased production, also violating the accord. Other producers that were once small and not necessarily part of the pact have since entered the game. In 1979, Malaysia produced 20,000 tons per year; now it produces more than 200,000 tons.[3] In other words, cacao producing countries failed to come to a collective agreement. Deforestation losses in Malaysia and the Ivory Coast were as dramatic as their gains in cacao production. Increased deforestation for cacao resulted in diminishing returns across the globe. With a low international price, all these countries, along with their forests, became losers. I don't recall the price of candy dropping since I was a child. Nestlé wins.

The price drop on global markets coupled with distributors' cartel buying has turned cacao production from a lucrative business into a money-losing venture.

Distributors cite two reasons in their defense. First, the price of cacao dropped while the costs of transportation remained fixed or increased. Due to these low prices, Amazonian distributors argue that unless they take a greater percentage of the sales to cover the cost of transportation, they will go out of business. Regardless, said colonists and agricultural technicians at CEPLAC, distributors make inordinate profits because of cartel buying.

Second, distributors claim that the quality of cacao from the Amazon was lower than that of the Northeast. This claim is hard to sustain, considering that the trees in Amazonia are genetically superior to those of the Northeast. The quantity of cocoa butter is higher per kilo of Amazonian beans, giving a higher percentage of chocolate per kilo of primary product. According to CEPLAC officials, when Amazonian cacao is properly processed, it is of higher quality than that of the Northeast.

However, quality declines in the Amazon due to mediocre processing by small producers. Processing involves picking the fruit, pulling out the slimy seeds (cocoa beans), fermenting them, and drying them in the sun before selling them to distributors. To produce better cacao, farmers must put more time and labor into the fermentation and drying processes. In addition, the witch's broom fungus, which infects cacao groves along the Transamazon, damages the beans. Distributors expect colonists to discard diseased fruit in the processing. Yet distributors have no quality control standard, as they have in the Northeast. That standard establishes a lower price for a poor quality cacao and a higher price for well-processed, high quality cacao. The cartel of distributors simply pays one low price for all Amazonian cacao, with few exceptions (discussed below). They sell the low quality cacao on the internal, Brazilian chocolate market. Higher quality cacao is exported. Swiss chocolate makers do demand well-processed cacao and are willing to pay for it. Since colonists are paid poorly no matter what the quality of their product, they have little incentive to spend more time in their processing or to throw out the diseased cacao. Thus, the distributors' claim that Amazonian small farmers produce a low quality cacao becomes a self-fulfilling prophecy.

Some producers have been able to obtain a better price through special deals with distributors by selling a higher quality product in bulk quantities. If a single farmer can produce 10,000 kilos of high quality beans, the distributors can send a whole truckload of their high quality cacao at once. Those farmers able to produce in bulk, therefore, take greater care in picking and invest in better processing equipment in order to improve their product. Producers of smaller quantities of cacao have not been able to successfully entice distributors into such deals, even with the highest quality product.

Recently, small producers found a way to address the price and quality disparity. By pooling their resources, small producers can amass bulk quantities to sell distributors at higher prices. Amazonian small producers have formed "associations" to make deals with distributors. They modeled their associations after the powerful producers' cooperative organizations in Brazil's Northeast. One reason for the high prices in the Northeast is the strength of small producers' cooperatives. These cooperatives inspect the cacao and demand higher prices from distributors for a well-processed product.

Amazonian associations are legally similar to cooperatives except that they are not taxed or regulated. Cooperatives must pay 17 percent state tax and 2.5 percent to FUNRURAL (Foundation for the Aid and Welfare of Rural Workers) for all products they sell. Associations have no established constitution and no "bureaucratic norms" set in Brasília by which they must abide.

An entrepreneurial small producer started an association in 1987 but initially failed to achieve sufficient membership to secure any leverage with distributors in collective bargaining. However, with the continued low price of cacao, small producers came to see the necessity of collective action. The month I arrived, that small producers' association sold 40,000 kilos to the distributor DISPAM, for U.S.$0.50 per kg., 50 percent above the Amazonian market price.

Some cooperatives in the Northeast became strong enough and large enough to buy their own trucks to transport and market the cacao themselves, bypassing intermediaries like Eduardo and his company. While I was in the Amazon, one association adopted this approach. It rented a truck and sent 10,000 kilos of cacao to the Northeast, earning U.S.$0.70 per kg. after transportation costs—double the Amazonian market price. Thus they obtained higher prices and proved the distributors' claims false. Their success encouraged other producers to organize. In the summer of 1989, two associations in the Altamira-Médicilandia region were in the process of being legally chartered by the government.[4] The choke-hold of the distributor's cartel slips as colonists organize themselves.

The growth of cooperation and collective action is not unique to cacao growers, nor is it new to the Transamazon. Colonists engaged in collective action almost from the outset, but their organizations did not always take the same form. Some began as grassroots movements among colonists, while others were brought in and even imposed by the government. Government versus privately initiated cooperative movements should be compared in their origins and efficacy in order to examine implications for future development.

Cooperation from Below: The Case of Side Road 27

Colonists engage in collective action because they share collective interests. Certain issues—road accessibility, education, health, agricultural techniques, and prices for agricultural products—are crucial for all colonists. Colonists on Side Road 27 have organized to improve all of these, beginning with the road itself.

Side roads are the colonists' lifeline to the highway and the outside world. One downed bridge can close a road, or forest invasion can turn it into a footpath. If it is closed to vehicle access, colonists are unable to transport large quantities of produce to market or to bring fertilizers and seedlings to their lots. Cut off from the market, colonists are forced into subsistence farming and possibly into debt to creditors who supply their basic needs for tools, medicines, seeds, and other necessities. In addition, colonists need road access to reach a hospital in an emergency. With only a footpath, a sick person must be carried out to the highway on a mule or someone's back. That can be a fifty-kilometer trek on some side roads. Seu Ricardo da Souza, the man who sold forty cows for his emergency operation, would never have made it out of the side road alive had he been carried the ten kilometers to the road by mule rather than by the family's Jeep.

Colonists also want access to basic education and health services on their own roads, not in some *agrovila* twenty-five kilometers away. With a population of five hundred on Side Road 27, colonists did not think their demands unreasonable. Neither did the government in 1970; it promised to maintain roads and deliver these health and educational services. However, between 1970 and 1980, the government provided fewer and fewer ser-

Mother and baby: a mother walks her child eight kilometers out of Side Road 27 to reach the health post in the *agrovila* on the highway—over twenty kilometers round trip, baby in tow.

vices until, by 1980, INCRA had virtually abandoned the region. Increasingly, colonists had to rely on each other, rather than the government, for survival.

Emilio Moran had warned me to expect that side roads would be closed two to three months of every year during the rainy season—they had been in 1973, when government support for the region was at its peak. The government was slow in fixing the highway; side roads had an even lower priority. Side roads are universally described in studies as extremely run-down due to government neglect, with bridges knocked out and areas where the forest has encroached, making roads impassable for cars and trucks. Colonists at the end of the side roads have access to their lots only by footpath. *Não têm condições* to keep them open, Eduardo had said.

I was, therefore, struck by the condition of Side Road 27. Like the highway, this road had potholes and erosion ditches, but nowhere had the forest turned it into a footpath and nowhere had the road completely washed away. Sturdily constructed bridges with no missing beams spanned every creek crossing. Next to these often lay the remains of a former bridge with its beams strewn on the creek's banks and in the water. Though the rainy season was just ending, the entire length was passable by large vehicles. In light of all the stories about run-down side roads, this seemed unusual.

So one of my first questions for the colonists was why? Why was this side road in such good condition? The answer: colonists on Side Road 27 fixed the road and bridges themselves. Before 1980 the government, through INCRA, kept the roads open. What INCRA had done before, colonists on Side Road 27 now did themselves. Since 1980, when colonists have needed to get something done, they have called a *reunião*, a "get-together" of all the men of the road, to solve the problem. INCRA still offers the use of a tractor every two years to keep the road clear of forest invasion, but the colonists must pay for the tractor's diesel fuel. This the colonists do willingly and would like to do more often. One tractor every two years does not maintain the road in good condition. Forest invasion can close a road within a year.[5]

To keep Side Road 27 open, families took responsibility for maintaining the 400 meters of road in front their own lots—clearing the weeds and filling potholes and ditches with rocks to prevent more erosion. When a bridge washes out, the men hold a *reunião* at the downed bridge. They select strong hardwood trees from lots near the bridge, cut them down, and with chain saws form the logs into one-by-one-foot beams, sometimes forty or fifty feet in length—an amazing feat, considering the size of hardwood trees and the difficulty in cutting hardwood with a chain saw. Colonists take great pride in saying that before 1980 INCRA took two to three months to fix a knocked out bridge; now the bridge is rebuilt, and the road is open within two or three days, without bureaucratic mess and delay. *Agora, é melhor porque faz logo*, one colonist told me, "It's better now because we do it right," using high-quality lumber and careful construction. They claim that their bridges last longer than INCRA's. None had fallen yet. Thus, the enormous task of maintaining a twenty-kilometer stretch of road in a rainforest became manageable through collective action.

On Side Road 27, colonist initiative actually began before 1980. In 1974, after the first oil crisis, colonists were already unhappy with Transamazonian development. Moran described bureaucratic nightmares while he lived there, lamenting a "structure of decision making which is insensitive to micro-level variability and has a tendency to homogenization of both environmental and social variables."[6] Moran and his former neighbors believed that diminishing resources were being poorly allocated and managed by bureaucratic planners who were out of touch with the realities faced by colonists. When families moved from the *agrovilas* to their lots, they lost the benefits of *urbanismo-rural*. Their children no longer had convenient access to the educational and health services provided in the *agrovila*. Although the *agrovila* scheme was well intentioned, government planning simply did not conform to colonist needs. Colonists wanted health posts on the side roads which could administer vaccinations for their children and dispense emergency medicines for common diseases such as malaria and dysentery. They needed primary schools with four years of education so that their children could learn to read and write. Unlike people on most side roads, colonists on Side Road 27 had achieved many of their goals. Why, I wondered, did things turn around for Side Road 27 and not other side roads? I happened to live with one answer to my question.

Just as Seu Melquiades felt that farmers could help each other become better farmers by sharing ideas and experience, so he also thought that they could help each other maintain roads and build schools by pooling their resources. The problems which all side roads encountered prompted Seu Melquiades to walk from house to house in 1974 to call the first *reunião*. In the *reunião* the colonists decided to submit a petition to INCRA demanding that a school be built on Side Road 27. A school is simply a one room building for thirty students and a teacher with an eighth grade education. INCRA agreed to the demands and built the first school on the side road. After a similar *reunião* in 1977, a second school was built. But those were the good old days "when INCRA was INCRA," as the colonists put it, and the government had the resources, the *condições*, to build schools. When colonists needed something in the 1970s, they petitioned the paternalistic government.

When the colonists asked for a third school in 1980, the government refused to build it. This time colonists called a *reunião*, pooled their labor and resources, and built a school themselves. The government then provided a small salary for the teacher. Now every child on Side Road 27 has relatively easy access to primary education—none walk more than six kilometers. Virtually every young adult who grew up on the road went to one of these schools and received three or four years of schooling.[7] Although he couldn't solve problems for every side road on the highway, Seu Melquiades realized his actions could make a difference on one side road—his own.

Securing access to health services is a continuing struggle for colonists on the frontier. Families on Side Road 27 complained that lack of access to health services was their greatest burden. One morning I passed a woman walking toward the highway carrying a cherubic baby in her arms and an umbrella to protect the baby from the sun. She had to walk eight kilometers out to the highway, catch a ride to the health post in the *agrovila*, then hitch and walk all the way back in order to have her baby treated.[8] As I passed her again walking home at the end of the day, she looked exhausted. The walk had taken her away from her many other vital activities as the *Dona* of a farm. In May 1989, just before my arrival, members of the community held a *reunião* and petitioned the government for the establishment of a health post on Side Road 27. Colonists were willing to build it, but the government had not agreed to stock it with medicines or to provide a visiting nurse. Colonists will keep up their efforts for a health post, and they had hopes that the newly elected government of President Fernando Collor would help more than the military's corrupt legacy, President José Sarney and his government. Considering the mess in which the Collor government found itself, the colonists would be better off relying on each other than on their government.

Frontier Democratization: The Case of *Agrópolis Brasil Novo*

Collective action has grown throughout the region. One shining example of colonists' community spirit and organization may be found at the *Agrópolis Brasil Novo*, 46 kilometers east of Altamira.[9] Under the PIN scheme, several *agrovilas* were administered by a regional *agrópolis*. As an administrative headquarters, the *agrópolis* community received preferential treatment during the 1970s. INCRA took care of its own. INCRA even provided electricity and running water for the houses of bureaucracy officials.

After INCRA's pullout in 1980, Brasil Novo began to fall apart. The water tower broke, and nobody fixed it. The electrical generator died. The town held a *reunião* and decided to set up a government with a popularly elected "director," then levied taxes on each household. The new government provides electricity and running water to every house in town—not just those of the administrators. Citizens of Brasil Novo proudly state that living standards for regular folks are better now than they were under INCRA. Even so, the old ways remain ingrained in Brasil Novo, as they do almost everywhere on the frontier. Colonists there remain nostalgic for the days of INCRA. They used the terminology of a bureaucracy, not a democracy, to name their headman. Paternalism runs deep in Brazilian political culture. However, Side Road 27 is clearly not alone in its success in breaking from the paternalistic tradition.

The transition from government direction of colonization to grassroots organization has been remarkable along the Transamazon Highway. Everywhere I stopped, I heard tales of change since the days of INCRA. Nowhere were those changes more visible than at Kilometer 92, where the CIRA-PACAL cooperative operates. PACAL illustrates some of the colonists' nightmares and triumphs resulting from the government pullout from colonization.

Cooperation from Above: The CIRA-PACAL Sugar Project

The history of government-sponsored cooperatives is strikingly different from the grassroots collective action that grew up on Side Road 27. In the early days of colonization, cooperatives were organized by the government, just like everything else. Each regional division of INCRA on the Transamazon was required to set up a CIRA (United Cooperative of the Agrarian Reform). These government-sponsored cooperatives were to assist colonists in everything from educating producers to storing, processing, and transporting products. Establishing cooperatives, like land reform, may seem antithetical to a bureaucratic-authoritarian regime. Stephen Bunker explained the military government's reasoning:

> Cooperatives provide an ideal vehicle for an income-concentrating capitalist regime's search for political legitimacy. With their emphasis on egalitarian participation, direct representation, member education, and collective solutions to commercial exploitation, they allow the regime which supports them to give the appearance of siding with the small, poor, direct producers against wealthier businessmen who benefit from their labor. The cooperative itself, however, implies no change in the regime of private property or in the distribution of land. . . . To the extent that the cooperative actually increases production and commerce of agricultural goods, it serves the state's interests at little political cost.[10]

Few of the cooperatives established by the military government increased production and commerce. The government-sponsored cooperative movement had, in Bunker's words, "the enduring problems of instant organization."[11] Since cooperatives were formed and largely run by government agencies rather than by colonists themselves, colonists had little stake in the success or failure of the organizations. Embezzlement and mismanagement plagued the cooperatives from the beginning, along with cutbacks in the support initially promised by the government.[12] Consequently, many failed soon after they were created, and colonists lost the money which they had put into the cooperatives as dues. Today, long after most of these failures, cooperatives continue to have a bad reputation on the Transamazon.

Due to peculiar circumstances, however, the CIRA-PACAL cooperative at Kilometer 92 survived and is currently growing stronger. Its story illustrates the problems of government-run cooperatives and the strength they can gain from grassroots initiative.

In the area 80 to 100 kilometers east of Altamira on the highway, soils are particularly fertile, and the terrain is relatively flat—one of the few places in Amazonia that is suited to intensive, mechanized agriculture. Here, next to *Agrovila Abraham Lincoln* at Kilometer 90, the government decided in 1972 to build its showcase development project: a modern sugar refinery in the middle of Amazonia. The project became known as PACAL (Agroindustrial Sugarcane Project of Abraham Lincoln). Near the sugar mill, a lumber mill was established to process the lumber cleared from colonists' lots. The colonists on the most fertile and flat lots were encouraged to join the CIRA, a cooperative of colonists who would produce the cane to be processed in the mill. These colonists were offered massive technical support, along with attractive loans to finance clearing their lands, planting the cane, and buying the heavy machinery to harvest and transport it.[13]

From the beginning the sugar mill seemed more of a public relations coup than an effort toward long-term regional development. The military government gave the new refinery national publicity. The refinery had its own airstrip that could bring in bigwigs and the media for special tours. The airstrip also brought the technicians from São Paulo and the bureaucrats from Brasília needed to run the refinery. To house all these people, INCRA built the well-appointed company town where I stayed. PACAL was designed as the ideal colonization development project: from clearing colonists' land, processing the lumber, and helping them produce sugar cane to refining it and selling the sugar in the Amazon and the hardwoods on national and international markets. With an original price tag reported at U.S. $6 million for construction of the refinery alone (in 1977 dollars), they spared little expense.[14]

Then the problems began. Contractors building the refinery reportedly took advantage of INCRA's ignorance and bought at a discount parts that did not fit or were out of date, then skimmed the savings as profit. They even located the refinery on top of a large hill so that it could be seen from the highway. Yet sugar refining requires huge water supplies. At PACAL, water must be pumped uphill to the mill, making it naturally inefficient. All other refineries in Brazil are located where water can flow down to them. That left colonists with the ultimate irony: an industry in Amazonia without adequate water supplies.[15]

The combination of errors resulted in a drop in the refinery's actual capacity to three-fifths of the original design and frequent breakdowns during harvest when rapid production was crucial. Parts had to be flown in from the South or Northeast to fix it.[16] With its frequent breakdowns during harvest, cane already cut was not always refined. Sugarcane must be burned in the field, then harvested, transported, and refined within a seventy-two hour period. Subtract the time needed for harvesting and transporting after burning, and little room is left for error at the mill. Much cane was wasted, decaying in trucks as the refinery sat idle.

The mill would have operated below capacity until 1980 regardless because colonists could not produce enough cane. Colonists had difficulty clearing and planting their fields at a rate sufficient to satisfy the mill's needs when it functioned. To increase the area of cane planted, PACAL used bulldozers to clear colonists' forest reserves, charging colonists for the bulldozer by the hour.[17] Bulldozers compacted the soils, resulting in lower yields than in areas cleared by hand. PACAL bought the hardwoods it cleared from the fields and processed the trees in its lumber mill. When colonists finally did produce a crop, they had difficulty finding workers to harvest the cane. Since labor is scarce on the frontier, and harvesting sugarcane is labor-intensive, work crews were brought in from the impoverished Northeast at astounding transportation costs.

Though the mill operated at an incredible loss with all these problems, the three INCRA directors, who lived in Brasília and commuted to the project, used the project's high profile and their extensive connections to secure continued financial resources from the government and from banks.

Those colonists able to produce sugarcane became relatively wealthy from the subsidies, amassed capital equipment, and bought more lots. Colonists who were not so lucky to have the flat terrain (less than 15 percent slope) and fertile soils requisite for cane growing resented INCRA's preferential treatment of PACAL and the CIRA cooperative members. The project received enormous amounts of money while the roads, the schools, other crops, and other cooperatives received little or no support. Many bureaucrats within INCRA saw their own low-cost programs wither while money was wasted on PACAL.

By 1979, INCRA wanted to wash its hands of the project despite the pleas of PACAL's directors. With 3,000 hectares of cane finally planted, the project was viable, and INCRA sold it at a discount to a powerful cooperative from the South which then sold the refinery to a private company, Conan, in 1981. In 1982, colonists cut their cane and brought it to the mill where it was processed. But according to colonists, Conan did not have the resources to run it. Conan went bankrupt that year, shut the mill, and never paid the producers for their cane.

Many colonists lost everything they had amassed up to that point—their cane fields, tractors, and trucks. Some sold their lots and moved on. The government-organized CIRA cooperative fell apart. In order to survive, other colonists resorted to collective action—something they had learned more through their side road communities than through the government-run cooperative.

CIRA members held a *reunião* in 1983 and decided to take action which would refocus government attention on the Transamazon. They blockaded the highway with their tractors and trucks, closing it for a month and forcing the government, through INCRA, to compensate them for the cane taken by Conan. In 1984, the Bank of Brazil tried to collect loans made to sugar producers in the late 1970s and early 1980, before interest rates went up with the debt crisis and before the mill went bankrupt. Colonists struck again, this time occupying and closing the bank's local branch. Again, INCRA bailed them out, paying their loans to the bank. Colonists wanted more than a bailout; they wanted the mill reopened.

They decided that action within the region would accomplish nothing. In a centralized bureaucratic state, the colonists would have to take their demands to the heart of the bureaucracy. In July 1985, the colonists drove in a convoy of trucks all the way to Brasília and parked in front of the Ministry of Agriculture. After thirty-five days of protesting, their demands were met. In 1986, INCRA resumed control of PACAL and reopened the mill. PACAL is the one project in the region where the role of INCRA has been resuscitated.

The cooperative side of the operation is no longer run on the line-and-staff, bureaucratic model of organization. Now colonists have a greater involvement in PACAL and in the many activities offered by the cooperative. The CIRA cooperative was legally reorganized in 1986—this time on the colonists' initiative, not the government's. It now has 270 member families. They hold meetings (*reuniões*) every other month with 80 percent of the members attending. Before 1980, members told me, such meetings practically did not exist.

The new cooperative takes collective action much like the community on Side Road 27 but on a broader scale. In the summer of 1989, one of the large bridges on the highway was too weak to handle the heavily laden cane trucks during harvest, so the cooperative repaired it. As a region-wide group of successful (if subsidized) farmers, the cooperative has the *condições* which most groups in the Amazon lack.

The cooperative also provides social services. CIRA runs three supermarkets which give members a 5 percent discount. The supermarkets use cooperative-owned trucks to buy goods in São Paulo and Belém, bypassing distributors. As for health care, where the community on Side Road 27 failed due to a lack of financial resources, the relatively wealthy cooperative runs its own health post, complete with a nurse, where members pay only 35 percent of market value for care and medicine. They had been looking for a doctor for three months but could attract none to the frontier, though they offered a salary three times higher than those paid in Belém. CIRA also acts as a welfare society for the poor. On Saturday mornings, the cooperative provides use of its trucks to the poor, landless workers of Médicilandia who then collect food donations from more prosperous farmers.

I learned most of this in an interview with the cooperative's current president and several current members. They said that if the PACAL mill could run at capacity and earn a profit in 1989, INCRA would turn it over to the colonists this time rather than sell it to an outside corporation. The CIRA planned to take control of the mill within one to three years. With all these accomplishments, I would have expected much more pride and boasting, but they all seemed wary of the future. Things had been going well for them in 1980, they said . . . just before the mill shut down. Though the cooperative now enjoys the vigor of member participation it never had before 1980, its survival still depends on the mill. The mill's continued success, according to almost all accounts, remains tenuous.

I lived with the technicians and the bureaucrats during my week-long stay at the project. The young on-site director from Brasília, Rapaz, headed the lumber end of the operation. He and the technicians offered their perspectives on the PACAL project and on the new CIRA cooperative. The mill, they said, needed massive amounts of capital to replace parts broken and rusted after sitting idle for so long. This time the government would not pour money into the project. As a result, the refinery is run more like a business than a showpiece.

In order to finance the restoration, PACAL increased its rate of cutting lumber. From January to July 1989, the lumber operation alone cleared $1.2 million in profits, all of which reportedly went back into the sugar refinery. PACAL had cleared the most valuable stands of hardwoods in the cooperative's region by the summer of 1989. To compensate, PACAL was ceded a nearby area of 60,000 hectares (600 square kilometers) full of valuable lumber to feed the refinery's appetite for cash. The new area was once inhabited by the Arara tribe, who have consistently had their lands invaded during the colonization process.[18] Environmental ramifications are clear. When profit margins are squeezed and capital is unavailable, Amazonian individuals and corporations turn to abundant natural resources to stay afloat, often with the government's blessing. With continued use, those resources disappear.

PACAL's environmental practices have improved on some scores. Rather than discarding the potassium-rich bagasse (the burned cane by-product of the refining process), they now use it to fertilize the fields. Bagasse recovery has an added environmental dimension. The water used in the refining, which is hot and full of the organic material known as bagasse, is now cooled in recovery ponds to allow the bagasse to settle. Before, this bagasse, with its high biodegradable oxygen demand (BOD), was pumped straight into the river. The bagasse would take up all the oxygen in the river. Deprived of oxygen, the fish died, leaving those dependent on local fisheries (not members of the cooperative) hungry. With the recovery ponds, this problem has apparently been ameliorated.

Towers of steel: a manager from Brasília, stands before one of four furnaces at PACAL's Agroindustrial Sugarcane Project, its sugarcane refinery near the Agrovila Abraham Lincoln, 92 kilometers west of Altamira.

Environmental protection: a PACAL technician from São Paulo stands in front of a settling pond for the PACAL surgarcane refinery. These ponds provide time for organic bagasse from the sugar-refining process to settle and decompose so that wastewater does not take up all the oxygen in nearby rivers. Settling ponds were created after local anglers complained of fish die-offs from wastewater.

In regards to their lumber practices, sustainable logging has yet to be achieved by a large forestry outfit in any rainforest, due to the delicate ecological setting and destructive logging practices.[19] However, certain forms of logging are less damaging than others. Rapaz made a deal with a German lumber importer who gave him the money to buy a special tractor which is not as damaging when taking out the trees as the D-8s previously used. The newer tractor drags trees out with a winch rather than bulldozing a road right to the tree, as is more common. PACAL is unique among Amazonian lumber companies in that it cannot simply exploit an area and move on. Its directors feel a long-term responsibility toward the local population of CIRA members and their Transamazon community. Rapaz said that he lobbied the government for an export tax on lumber which would go toward researching ways to replant mahogany and other hardwoods. The tax (less than 5 percent) was put into place last spring. He was aware of and regretted the ecological consequences of the logging, but he felt he had no choice if the sugar refinery was to remain open.

Rapaz and I talked about the cooperative's plans to take over the refinery. He said that the colonists would assume legal control of it within a year or two. The Brasília directorate would formally occupy an advisory role but still maintain de facto control because the directors say that colonists cannot manage the operation themselves. Nor will the refinery run without its highly educated technicians, all of whom come from the South. When I asked if people from the region would ever be able to run it themselves, Rapaz replied, "Realistically? No. We tell them what to do, and they do it." The educational infrastructure in the Amazon is weak; a colonist receiving a secondary education is lucky, and the closest university is 1,000 kilometers away by dirt road (the highway). None of the colonists and few of their children will ever have the technical education necessary to run a sugar mill. The president of the cooperative, a colonist himself, agreed that the directors give most of the orders. None expect the umbilical cord of management and technical assistance from the South to be severed in the foreseeable future.

Many dilemmas of Amazonian development became painfully clear in my study of PACAL. As we toured the poorest workers' quarters, Rapaz explained that the hardship was unavoidable, cooperative or no cooperative. This was a business and had to be run like a business. "In development," he said, "some of the people have to be forgotten, some have to die for the growth of the others." As he was saying this, one of the mill workers' wives came up to us with a baby boy who had been severely burned on most of his body a week earlier by boiling cooking oil. Rapaz put her and the baby into the "President's Car" (three different military presidents had ridden in the old Chevy Suburban during the 1970s, when the government had used the project in annual appeals for populist legitimacy). While we drove to the health post, he kept talking. "My father gave me some advice that is painful but true: You can't run a business with your heart. You must run it with your mind." At the health post he paid for the baby's treatment and the medicine. He said that one-third of his salary goes to helping people in the project. He had inherited money and did not need it like these people did. When they are in trouble, they come to him.

He chose to work for PACAL because he believed in it. "My friends in Brasília tell me, 'Man, you are destroying the Amazon with that lumbering.' I tell them that's true, and I'm sorry about that. But there are 300 families involved in this project, and I know that I am helping them." He talked about the nuns lending trucks to the poor on Saturdays. "In the South, I face starving people on the streets every day. They may be poor here, but nobody goes hungry."

Many of the colonists echoed this sentiment. I once hitched a ride atop a truck full of produce. An order of nuns runs a house for needy mothers in Altamira. The nuns' truck visits all the side roads on a rotating basis and requests food donations from farmers. Though many of the farmers are very poor themselves, most give, they told me, because they know that they have land and that some people are even poorer than themselves. The co-operative helps ensure that every family in Médicilandia has food.

Rapaz's father is right. Businesspeople do run businesses with their minds—to turn a good profit. That profit is often extracted through the suffering of human beings and the environment . . . hence the rise of labor unions, hence the Green Party movement, hence cooperatives. The cooperative movement calls the whole profit-oriented mentality into question. While Rapaz's father and his own reason demand that he run CIRA-PACAL as a business, and while the surrounding region is degraded, Rapaz's conscience will not allow those he sees in need to be forgotten. Cooperatives are created to work toward the good of the many, not the élite.

Some members of the cooperative did not like the way PACAL was being run and certainly resented the control exercised by the Brasília directorate. They felt resources were being misdirected. In the end, sugar producers have profited from all the money pumped into the project and from the lumber operation which fells a formerly communal forest and have become something of an élite in the region. Others have been left out. In the 1970s, CIRA had nothing to do with anything but sugarcane. After the breakdown of the early 1980s, sugar producers realized they could not rely on a single

crop for their livelihood. Many diversified their crop base and are concerned over the prices of products such as cacao, pepper, and coffee, along
with the staples rice, beans, corn, and manioc. These cultivars have been
the mainstays of the majority of colonists in other parts of the highway all
along. Some cane producers have recognized the skewed support given to
the PACAL project. This has created a political rift within the cooperative.

Some members want CIRA to expand its membership and commercial
interests to aid producers of other crops, such as cacao. Similar rumblings
arose over CIRA's role in the late 1970s, when some colonists and certain factions within INCRA proposed the combination of CIRA with
COOPERFRON, a broader based cooperative with more popular support.
PACAL's powerful Brasília directorate subverted the proposal's fruition
back then.[20] The current directorate is more favorable to expanding the
role of CIRA-PACAL. The group already owns several trucks and is ex-
porting lumber. With access to transportation and international markets,
colonist producers could bypass distributors altogether, cutting out the intermediaries, in order to earn global export prices. CIRA supporters and
critics agree that other producers would be helped by CIRA; now it is a
question of when CIRA's elected administration will be ready to enter these
other areas. The president of the cooperative expects it within a year
or two.

Other colonists who were left out of the sugar bonanza entirely are fun-
damentally opposed to the project's existence. Though PACAL is supposedly an Amazonian project, sugarcane was being cut by labor imported
from the Northeast, refined by a mill and technicians imported from the
South, and managed by a bureaucracy from Brasília. With a price tag well
above $10 million by 1989 for the refinery alone, the opportunity costs of
this project for Amazonian development have been staggering. The ecological costs to the rainforests from bulldozing lots and continued logging
have been disastrous. Many colonists were asking, "Is this development?"

How much independence CIRA can exercise in the future remains to be
seen. Today, members are politically active and participate in making decisions and running the cooperative—markedly different from the days
when it was run entirely by INCRA. Back then, colonists played the pawns
in a military government's grand political quest for legitimacy. Those days
of swelled budgets are over. An invigorated cooperative and an embattled
directorate have learned from past mistakes and are determined to make
the operation viable and the region prosperous.

Implications for Future Development and Land Reform

Colonists are divided on the benefits and drawbacks of the government's original colonization scheme and its declining role in the region. During the early 1970s when Latin American governments could easily attract international financing through low-interest loans (often with negative real interest), many sponsored colonization programs to open up areas which had been depopulated or "underpopulated" since the arrival of Europeans. Most of these schemes became financial and environmental catastrophes.

In 1973, as these projects continued full steam, Michael Nelson discussed the advantages of spontaneous colonization over government-sponsored projects: "Few spheres of economic development have a history of, or reputation for, failure to match that of government-sponsored colonization in humid tropical zones."[21] Nelson described the low "internal rate of return" of these government-sponsored schemes versus the less capital-intensive spontaneous colonization. Spontaneous colonization begins with individual initiative and fosters self-reliance and community solidarity, which are essential in a frontier environment. In the 1980s, colonists showed themselves to be more efficient in organizing themselves than INCRA ever was.

In the long run, many of the well-intentioned, paternalistic government programs have proven detrimental in fostering the colonists' learned helplessness. INCRA tried numerous ways of creating community spirit, from mothers' clubs and weekend dances to forming and funding cooperative organizations. But the colonists had little incentive to take part in collective action when the government would provide everything for them. Some do not accept that those days are over. They await a new government, a new INCRA, to arrive as savior. Those waiting do not share in Side Road 27's success. Their roads become footpaths, and their farmers produce for subsistence.

The president of the CIRA cooperative spoke of apathy in the region during an interview with me, saying, "Problems don't resolve themselves when people wait." Today many colonists choose to do things on their own through collective action rather than to rely on the government. The *reuniões*, associations, and cooperatives have changed the face of the Transamazon colonization. Though bureaucrats and technicians from the South question these uneducated colonists' abilities to run complex organizations by themselves, colonists are guardedly confident. They garner plenty of management experience from farming their 100 hectares on the frontier. Colonists welcome training and technical assistance but feel quite capable of running their communities and their businesses themselves.

A once hegemonic bureaucracy must adjust and is adjusting to the new order in Amazonia. In the 1970s, government agricultural technicians visited every farm to give individual advice in modern agricultural techniques. This was costly and time-consuming for the limited number of technicians. When funding for agricultural assistance dried up, these visits ended. Today, colonists are requesting that the technicians come to association meetings and side road *reuniões*. At meetings, the technicians teach the colonists as a group, and the colonists help each other improve agricultural techniques. They adapt to their ecosystem as a community and build cohesion in the process. By working through colonist organizations, the government efficiently achieves the same results as by visiting individual lots.

Grassroots organizations have improved the quality of their products while lowering the cost of government assistance in the production. One CEPLAC technician prefers this, saying, "Unfortunately, whatever the government tries to initiate usually fails. But now if something fails, colonists cannot blame CEPLAC or the government. They have to admit, 'The decision was mine.' "[22] What the government used to do at a high cost, colonists now do themselves with (in the words of game theorist Mancur Olson) the "coherence and efficiency of small groups."[23] This has freed government resources for other projects that may actually improve long-term prospects for regional and national prosperity.

The movement toward collective action has grown throughout the region, from the small side road communities to the officially recognized cooperatives and associations to the democratization of entire towns. The movement's force extends to organizations such as the Catholic church and Rural Workers' Unions with their national and international ties. These groups often organize the community on larger regional and national issues, such as equitable land distribution.

The Question of Land

In Amazonia, Indians, the Church, and the Rural Workers' Unions are demanding a reform of the PIN land reform—the redistribution of large landholders' lands as well as the demarcation of extractive reserves and Indian lands. The movement parallels community-based organizations like the associations, the cooperatives, and the side road *reuniões*, but on a regional and national scale. The Amazon is politically ripe for land reform, and Amazonians have amply demonstrated their ability to carry out these programs on the local level.

Access to land is a concern for all colonists. The 1970 PIN land reform succeeded in turning many landless and dispossessed families into yeomen farmers. These farmers fear that such opportunities will not exist for their children and grandchildren.

Colonist families often include five, six, or ten kids. One woman I met had had thirty-one pregnancies, twenty-two live births, and thirteen living children. Each of those thirteen children will someday want a lot of his or her own to raise a family. Seu Melquiades asked me, "How can thirteen kids fit on one lot?" I wondered to myself how five billion people can live on one planet. One solution to population pressure on land is, of course, birth control. Without dramatic changes in population policies and trends, Brazil's population will double sooner than Seu Melquiades might like to think, while pressures on land will rise exponentially.

With the "locals" demanding land along with a constant influx of the dispossessed from other parts of the country, the region has a growing number of *sem terras*, "the landless." Colonists have a natural compassion for the landless because most colonists themselves came to the frontier, not by choice, but out of necessity. They could not afford good land in their home states in the Northeast and South. Colonists who recognize the inequity of land distribution are banding together with the landless through the Rural Workers' Union over the issue of land reform.

Even on the frontier, where colonists claim, "There's plenty of land left," conflicts over land are common and violent. In Amazonia, if the landless do not become wage laborers, they become squatters, occupying untitled land and clearing it to stake their claims. But large landholders, whom colonists call *grilheros*, or "landgrabbers," can also acts as squatters. *Grilheros* often steal land from small squatter farmers. The *grilheros* pay workers to clear a tract of untitled forest and plant grass. Sometimes they put cows in the new pasture, sometimes they don't. Often *grilheros* simply cut a trail around the forest in a wide area, through forests claimed by small squatters. Whatever falls within the circle made by the trail, the *grilheros* claim as theirs. *Grilheros* then pay gunmen to guard their claim from the squatters whose lands they stole in the first place. When government agents come to survey the land, *grilheros* use their wealth to influence the surveyors.

Union hall: graffiti on the wall of the Rural Workers Union of Altamira reads
Kararaô = Morte e Destruição—"Kararaô = Death and Destruction." Kararaô,
a proposed dam project near Altamira, would flood the tribal lands after which it
was initially named. The dam project's name was later changed, though the project
remains on the table.

Near Médicilandia, one *grilhero* told the squatters, whose land he had
invaded, to settle on nearby lands demarcated for the recently contacted
and reunited *Arara* tribe. The *grilhero*, in tandem with a lumber company
that built a road into Arara lands, was kind enough to help the landless
squatters move to the Arara area. That way, the *grilhero* made available to
himself lands that could be legally settled by colonists. This pits the squatters against the Arara in a battle which could be won only by the *grilhero*. I
spoke with one squatter who had been moved to Arara lands. He said the
tribe had contacted him. A few Arara warriors arrived one day and handed
him an arrow, just to let him know where he stood. They made clear to him
that if he put anything permanent on their land which might give him claim
to it—a barn or a perennial crop—they would burn it down. But the Arara
understand the situation, as does the squatter.

The Arara have joined forces with the Rural Workers' Unions of Altamira and Médicilandia and the Catholic church to combat the landed interests. The church's alliance with workers and Indians reflects an historical shift in the church's approach to politics after the Second Vatican Council (1962–1965). Following the 1968 conference of Bishops at Medellín, Columbia, parts of the Catholic church in Latin America became radicalized. Some of its priests proclaimed the "theology of liberation," and many set up what were called *communidades evangelicos de base* (CEBs), grassroots peasant organizations. The movement espoused that the powerless cannot wait for others to give them power but must empower themselves. In the words of Paulo Freire, "The oppressed must be their own example in their struggle for redemption."[24]

The coalition of the Arara, Rural Workers' Union, and Catholic church have continually petitioned the government for restitution of both native and small farmer lands from this particular *grilhero*. The Arara agreed to give some of their land on the north side of the highway to colonists if the government demarcated and protected Arara land on the south side (along the Xingu River), as a legal reservation. The government agency MIRAD (which replaced INCRA) has been inordinately slow in responding to the demands of the coalition. Union officials and squatters believe that MIRAD acts in the *grilhero's* interest if it acts at all.

The rise of collective action among these three groups is not confined to the Altamira-Médicilandia region. Grassroots groups act all over Amazonia as watchdogs against large holder *grilhero* invasions and human rights abuses. The landed interests often respond with violence, by killing the leaders of a movement. The most notorious case is that of Chico Mendes, president of a Rural Workers' Union of rubber tappers of Xapuri in the state of Acre. Like the colonists of the Transamazon, the rubber tappers were having their lands invaded by rancher *grilheros*.

In the late 1970s, tappers began to organize *empates*, "stand-offs," against *grilhero* invasions. Members of the union would literally stand between the trees and the work crew which was paid to deforest the tappers' lands and were accompanied by gunmen.[25] The tactic worked so well that the *grilheros* often retaliated. Chico Mendes was shot and killed on December 22, 1988. Many rural leaders had died before Mendes and many have died since, but his death drew national and international attention to the violent plight of Native Americans, rubber tappers, and small farmers in the Amazon. Whether that attention and the international pressures on the government that it brought will translate into action on the part of the govern-

141

ment in addressing equitable land distribution has yet to be determined.

The designation of extractive reserves and native reservations was a step in the right direction but not necessarily a popular step in Brazil. The Collor government that established the reserves fell from power after a corruption scandal in 1992. What policies the current or future governments will enact is anyone's guess. Colonists, forest peoples, and the landless of the Amazon may become tired of waiting for the government to act and enact land redistribution themselves through land occupations and *empates*.

Of course, the large holders will protest. They are a powerful group in Amazonia and the rest of Brazil, and they regularly use coercion to maintain or increase their power. In some cases, force must be met with force, and criminals must be treated as criminals. That may sound simplistic and antagonistic, but governments ought to protect the innocent, not abet those who violate human rights.

Grassroots redistribution has its precedent in peasant land occupations throughout Latin America. In Central America, land occupations by peasant organizations (known alternately as land "reclamations" or "invasions") have been one of the primary means of balancing the unequal distribution of land.[26] The military governments of Central America equated peasant organizations and land invasions with Communist insurgencies and enlisted the financial and military assistance of the United States to conduct a war against them; not a precedent I would wish on Brazil.

Colonists of the Transamazon are hardly a left-leaning peasantry; if anything, they form a profoundly conservative yeomanry. Unlike peasants of Central America, these colonists have a strong interest in safeguarding property rights. But much like Central America, large holder's claims of rights to land are tenuous; few large holders ever work the vast lands they claim. What the government gave away, the government or colonists can take back. Seu Melquiades and others like him do not organize communist insurgencies; they launch insurgent democracies. The yeomanry build democratic structures which will serve Brazil well in its transition from military rule. If the development of a democratic society is the goal, equitable land distribution in the rural sector is an excellent means.

As the government withdrew its control and support on the frontier, the range of political options opened up for colonists, but the land tenure system remained in place. Politically, colonists created new, democratic forms of self-government based on mass participation, striving for ends that benefited all small farmers and, in some cases (like food donations for the poor), ends that benefited the landless.

In many ways, Amazonian development mirrors that of Brazil as a whole. Infusion of outside capital and technical assistance during the last three decades led to massive and rapid changes in the Amazon. Yet colonists had little control over that assistance. When external forces changed the policies of the metropolis, the assistance shrank. Colonists found themselves on the periphery of a system that was unresponsive to their needs. They turned to collective action to find the *condições* to resolve their crisis. Out of necessity, colonists began to do themselves what all the government bureaucrats and their fat budgets could never inspire them to do—they organized.

8

THE FUTURE FOR SMALL FARMERS IN AMAZONIA

Under the trees of Amazonia, a farmer picks his path amidst the branches and the bramble. Well below the canopy lies his garden and orchard within the forest. He finds a young tree and plucks an orange fruit the size of his thumb: taperebá. Birds have already picked at the ripe fruit in the upper branches. One taste tells him it's time for the harvest.

Choices that colonists have made over the last twenty years may seem irrational to environmentalists. Too often they cleared forests to plant pasture. On my first walk down Side Road 27, the landscape stretching before me seemed a haphazard jumble of forest and cacao groves, white sand and pasture, the strange and the familiar. Yet colonist choices are anything but random. With every farm tour, with every interview, colonist rationale became clearer to me.

Colonists and large holders alike make rational choices within the Amazonian context. They examine the variables that affect their production—their capital and labor resources, the possible cultivars given the quality of their soils and terrain, and the markets for those cultivars—then they deforest and plant accordingly. When forest reserves seemed limitless, one factor of the development equation was often ignored: deforestation's costs in land degradation and species destruction. Colonists have become painfully aware of these costs after having degraded some of their lands until they became unusable. Some colonists are attempting to undo their mistakes.

144

Another Sandman: a farmer peels skins off the manioc after it has soaked in water for days in the pit beside him. Like Sandman, he owns 100 hectares of white sand.

In the end, people moved to the frontier because their options in their old homes were narrowing. Now they are surrounded by land that is dying quickly, by a deteriorating economy, and by hostile banks. What are these people's options? Sandman is old; he will die before his land is exhausted; but he has four daughters and two sons. Together they will share one hundred hectares of sand in the middle of what was once a rainforest. With the land's few nutrients gone, it might support one hundred cows under optimal conditions for a limited time. But "optimal conditions" are nothing other than a theoretical possibility. Neighboring pastures with this number of cows suffered extensive erosion and soil compaction and were overrun by insects and aggressive second growth. Sandman's family is poor now, and their future is bleak.

While Sandman and his family attempt to eke out a living on poor soils, rich soils are wasted by medium and large holders who deforest to plant pasture, not crops, and sometimes never even put cows on the lands they clear. Large holders still treat the land and forests as if they were an unlimited resource. They have little, if any, incentive to leave forests intact. Brazil's "use it or lose it" laws encourage deforestation. As ranchers claim their lion's share of the bounty, as the government favors this crop or that, as colonists' children open the expansive but infertile lands, this pattern of land use will continue to repeat itself across the frontier unless the government's land distribution policies change.

One solution proposed herein would be a land redistribution carried out by colonists and forest peoples. The proposal would not deprive poor Brazilians of a living; it would help them avoid an agroeconomic dead end. Colonist small holders have the expertise to choose for redistribution those deforested lands which are best suited for intensive agriculture and those which are best suited for reforestation. Fertile areas already deforested should be colonized and cropped by small holders; infertile areas should be reforested; forested areas not yet controlled by ranchers or colonists should remain under the control of forest peoples. The government could implement a progressive land tax to discourage large holdings and continued deforestation. If stiff enough, the land tax could drive large holders to abandon deforested lands altogether. By default, the natural cycle of succession would reclaim the lands not occupied by small holders but abandoned by large holders. If some people were willing to engage in forest management on the infertile areas, secondary forest growth might yet be made more productive.

Colonists have shown themselves capable of carrying out such a redistribution. Not only do they have the ecological know-how, but they also have the political will and are developing the organizational skills necessary for the undertaking. Collectively, small farmers have come to understand and to work with their environment as no individual could. They have a long way to go before grasping the complexities and the possibilities of their forests.

Rainforests, in their natural state or with modest forest management, offer enormous possibilities for biotechnology and genetic engineering as well as continued production of fruit, nuts, herbs, fibers, pulp, lumber, and fish. Such potential should not be trampled under the hooves of cattle in a desperate, empty grab for short-term profits by Brazil's powerful elite. The human and environmental toll is simply too high. While deforesting and planting a monoculture of crops may sometimes provide food and a better standard of living in the short run, global warming, soil degradation, and the loss of biodiversity bring crisis in the long run.

Many colonists are beginning to recognize the failures of intensive agriculture. Continued monoculture cropping in the humid tropics requires more and more pesticides, herbicides, and fertilizers to maintain productivity, further degrading the environment. Like native peoples, colonists have taken to experimentation in order to adapt to their new environment. In adapting their practices to Amazonia's demands, colonists are in the rudimentary stages of creating an agricultural system similar to the one used by indigenous peoples for millennia. Part of the forest has been and will continue to be anthropogenic. A mix of uses—intensive agriculture, forest management and extraction, and preservation—are all appropriate in various niches, or vast expanses, of the Amazon.

Profiting from Biodiversity

Farmers all over the world are beginning to recognize the value of genetic diversity and the dangers of losing that diversity. Right now in my hometown of Sonoma, vineyards are being ravaged by biotype-B *phylloxera*, a tiny louse that attacks the roots of plants and damages them by impairing the absorption of nutrients. Afflicted vines stop growing and eventually die. Viticulturists (grape growers) must pull up and replace entire vineyards. The louse is native to the Americas. It migrated from wild vines in the Mississippi Valley to France and to California in the 1850s, shriveling vineyards in its path. It has attacked vines in waves ever since.[1] *Phylloxera* thrives in fine, clay soils like those of California's North Coast.

Lucky for the viticulturists, one of the premier agricultural research institutions of the world lies a mere hour's drive to the east, at the University of California at Davis. Davis researchers continually develop new *phylloxera*-resistant strains of vines through breeding and genetic engineering. Breeding and genetic engineering depend on a healthy gene pool. Before they can produce *phylloxera*-resistant vines, researchers must locate *phylloxera*-resistant genes. That may require a return to the Mississippi Valley in search of wild vines that developed a natural resistance to native pests. We of Sonoma hope that the Mississippi Valley's habitat hasn't been wiped out and the native plants driven to extinction.

Destruction of primeval habitat, be it rainforest or marshland, carries immense opportunity costs. Recent discoveries illustrate the value of species preservation in old growth forests in particular. Biotechnology firms have derived taxol, a cancer fighting drug, from the Pacific yew tree of the Pacific Northwest's old growth forests. The rosy periwinkle (*Catharanthus roseus*) of Madagascar yields the alkaloids vinblastine and vincristine which fight Hodgkin's disease and lymphocytic leukemia. Substances derived from the rosy periwinkle alone generate an income in excess of U.S.$100 million a year.[2]

Surprising as it may sound, biotechnology companies do not seem to place much value on biodiversity. American biotechnology companies lobbied against tropical nations sharing copyrights on the genetic material found in their unique ecosystems. The biotech industry does not wish to share their profits or technology with anyone. The Bush administration backed the companies' position and scuttled the biodiversity treaty at the 1992 Earth Summit in Rio de Janeiro. Such a myopic approach will have biotech researchers looking for the next Pacific yew or rosy periwinkle twenty years from now and finding a wasteland of monocultures where a genetic treasure trove once stood. Predictably, biologist Thomas Lovejoy advocates a more long-term view, "thinking about the problem as a joint venture in which both sides have property rights."[3]

Compromising on a biodiversity treaty would prevent compromising the forest. Colonist small farmers, and tropical countries as a whole, may see that maintaining genetic diversity is in their own interest if they share the rewards from biotechnology research. The world's greatest gene pool offers Brazil the world's largest competitive advantage in biotechnology, not to mention in agroforestry. The University of California at Davis became a premier research institution precisely because of its location in the heart of California's farm belt. Farmers provided a ready market for Davis' products and an opportunity for further research. The Amazon could spawn similar premier research institutes for biotechnology and agroforestry. The forest could provide the gene pool while the farmers could provide one market for the institutes' products. For that to happen, the United States must allow tropical countries to profit from what is rightfully theirs.

In Sonoma, we profit from biodiversity and from generations of experience with the ecosystem. Moderate winters, hot summers, and foggy mornings make my hometown conducive to grape growing. The climate and soils suit certain varietals. Viticulturists like Jim Bundschu know the various soil properties and plant accordingly. He told me that an isolated patch of white clay soils on four acres of his property produces award-winning Cabernet Franc grapes. If he had planted Gwürtztraminer there, the product might be mediocre. Europeans have practiced the art of viticulture for centuries. Bordeaux, Champagne, Alsace, the Rhine: various regions produce their distinctive wine varietals well-suited to their microclimates.

Agroforestry research: an EMBRAPA technician at the experimental station
23 kilometers west of Altamira inspects a mixed plantation of rubber, cacao,
and Brazil nut trees.

Not-so-sophisticated wine drinkers can tell the basic differences between
the wines of these regions. The subtle differences in microclimates, varietals, and processing of the grapes have resulted in centuries of enjoyment
and economic gain.

Like wine growers, Amazonians have historically adapted to local microclimates and local species. The *várzea* produced *açaí* fruit and heart of
palm; Brazil nuts grew in the *terra firme* of the Amazon basin; the Andes

region produced coca leaves and the tree bark for quinine. Indigenous peoples became incredibly specialized, adapting to the heterogeneity of their ecosystem by cultivating hundreds of different varieties of manioc and corn. Anthropologist Dominique Irvine reports that the Runa tribe of Ecuador commonly cultivate five to ten different varieties of manioc in the space of half a hectare to squeeze the most out of their soils and to vary the flavors and textures of their manioc.[4] Amazonia offers not simply varietals of one species for one industry, but varieties of a multitude of species for many industries. We must create and foster new markets for those industries, for Amazonian goods.

Part of the solution to Amazonia's crisis may lie here in America, in our consumption patterns. Amazonians consume an incredible variety of delicious fruits, most of which are not known even to people from São Paulo. *Paulistas* and Americans drink their Nestle's Quick every morning and say yes, please, to fresh ground pepper at restaurants, but scarcely do they imagine the Amazon's cornucopia. Would we rather eat beef and potatoes every night or a hundred different kinds of Amazonian fruits and nuts and, perhaps, a wild tapir now and then? The chocolate and black pepper markets have become increasingly saturated during the last ten years because these are two of the few rainforest products which Brazilians have successfully produced *and* marketed. Amazonian farmers and forest peoples should begin by supplying their own country, let alone the world, with the bounties of their harvest.

Our government can play an activist role in opening markets for forest products and in guaranteeing the continued health of those markets. Historically, once the rest of the world discovered a forest product (which often meant expanding the use of products that forest people had used for years) and demand grew, the cost of that product increased as supply was limited by what a forest could produce. Rather than relying on forest production, we have an economy which encourages farmers to clear those productive forests and plant the desirable product in a plantation monoculture. The most notorious case may be when the British secreted rubber tree seedlings from native stands in Brazil and began monoculture plantations in Southeast Asia. Once Malaysian rubber plantations began producing, the Brazilian rubber industry collapsed. It never recovered. Rubber tappers who rely on the forest cannot compete with rubber plantations. Rubber, cacao, pepper, and the rest show where that approach has led us—to a loss of biodiversity and to price collapses of formerly profitable forest products. As we "discover" new forest products we should consider buying those products exclusively from the forest people who collect them or perhaps from those who plant them in managed forests rather than on plantations. This may raise the cost to the consumer, but it will lower the rate of forest destruction for plantation agriculture.

A heightened awareness of the effects of deforestation and efforts to consume rainforest products in the United States have had a direct impact on the opening of markets and opportunities for more complex agroforestry and forest extractive industries. Susanna Hecht reports that, due to rising prices for forest products, some colonists have recently turned away from intensive agriculture and ranching in pursuit of agroforestry and forest extractive industries.[5] One cooperative of colonists near Porto Velho decided to convert their failed pastures into forest in an attempt to manage second growth for fruit production. Their venture has been backed to the tune of U.S.$500,000 by a Dutch group.[6] They hope that a market will exist for their fruits once the forest starts producing. Rather than colonists converting forests into colonized pasture lands, the Amazon may well convert colonist small farmers into forest people.

As markets for rainforest products open up, colonists will find that primary rainforests are more productive—in lumber, in medicines, and in protein—than the degraded pastures that have replaced them. Ecologists speak of biodiversity as a resource. That resource does little good for humanity unless someone can recognize and collect the valuable species. Forest peoples and colonists with generations of experience in the Amazon are themselves an invaluable human resource.

Colonists have an expression: *O governo fez o ocupação; nós fizemos a colonização*, "The government occupied; we colonized." They mean that the government built roads and brought people to the Amazon, but the colonists have settled the frontier, come to know it, made it theirs, and become a part of it. Five generations from now, small farmers on the Transamazon Highway may realize that certain species of cacao, or pepper, or other forest products produce well on their land, are resistant to local diseases, and taste better than what they planted previously. They will be able to experiment with and respond to the heterogeneity of the ecosystem because they will be intimately familiar with their particular valley or mountainside, their forest, their plot of soil. Adaptation takes time; the colonists have just begun.

NOTES

1. Amazonia: Why Cows?

1. Others have referred to the Transamazon as cutting across "virgin" or "primary" forests. A distinction will be drawn here between mature and primary. "Primary" implies a forest free from human alteration. "Mature" implies a fully grown forest, be it primary or anthropogenic.

2. Hecht and Cockburn 1989: 52.

3. Mahar 1989: 6–7.

4. Goodland and Irwin 1975: 26–30.

5. Posey 1983: 244–248.

6. Hecht and Cockburn 1989: 41.

7. Moran 1981; N. Smith 1982.

8. As will be discussed later, the actual number of the side road has been changed along with people's names in order to protect informants.

2. Dilemmas of Development

1. Brown 1978: 154, cited by N. Smith 1982: 75.

2. Davis 1978.

3. Schuh 1970, from Moran 1981: 226.

4. Bunker 1985: 80.

5. Drought sweeps over the Northeast on a cyclical basis. 1993 marks the fourth year of the new drought cycle, and once again poverty stricken Northeasterners are on the verge of starvation. This time, the old safety valves of Southern industrial work or Amazonian mining opportunities do not carry the appeal they once did, as unemployment now runs at 15 percent in São Paulo, and Amazonian mining camps have a reputation for slave conditions. (Brooke 1993.)

6. The expropriation also attempted to prevent land speculation. For a discussion of land speculation by small holders, see Moran's 1984 article "Social Reproduction in Agricultural Frontiers."

7. For various takes on the costs and benefits of the Grande Carajás program,

see "Amazônia: Onde Está a Verdade?" 1989; Fearnside 1986a; Hall 1986; Hecht and Cockburn 1989; Mahar 1989.

8. Bunker 1985: 82.

9. Smith 1982: 16, 20.

10. Mahar 1979: 27.

11. Moran 1981: 224.

12. Moran 1973–1974: 6.

13. Ibid.

14. Considering the low incidence of war over border disputes in Latin America, the military's fears seem to be unfounded.

15. I went hiking through the forest one day with three guys hunting peccaries. One hunter told me he was in the army: Special Forces Division, counter-insurgency. His job was jungle warfare. As we hacked our way past the various plants, he pointed to a tree covered in spines four to six inches long. "To beat the legs," he explained. They place spines on trip-wire, and when someone walks into it, the spines come up from out of the ground and stick into the legs. They contain a natural poison which paralyzes the legs and causes severe pain. As the child of some of the first Transamazonian colonists, this soldier grew up hiking through and getting to know these forests and their dangers. Apparently the military succeeded in drawing Amazonia into its strategic web.

16. N. Smith 1982: 23, quoting from article in *O Liberal*, Belém, October 5, 1974: 1.

17. Hecht and Cockburn 1989: 53 n.21.

18. Ibid., 147.

19. Simon Kuznets articulated this process in his inverted-U shaped curve analysis of capitalist development, though he did not argue that redistribution or continued growth was inevitable. (Kuznets 1955.)

20. Locke 1980: 21.

21. As the military government stepped down in the mid-1980s, it helped rewrite the Brazilian constitution. The new constitution mixed anachronistic land laws with some progressive clauses on native peoples' rights and provision of the right to vote for sixteen-year-olds. One Brazilian lawyer I met gave the new constitution mixed reviews, describing it as "older than the old constitution."

22. Hecht and Cockburn 1989: 118.

23. Cronon 1983: 122–123.

24. Hecht and Cockburn 1989: 211. Hecht gave the figure of 5,000 Indians in 1920. Krenak gave the figure as "more than 2,000" (personal communication).

25. Ibid., 218.

26. Posey 1989. See also Posey 1983; and an interview with him in Hecht and Cockburn 1989, Appendix B. For discussion of Huastec Mayan forest management, see Alcorn 1984.

27. Hecht and Cockburn 1989: 214.

28. Ibid., 12.

29. Goodland 1975: 30.

30. Lovejoy 1983: 211–213.

31. Figures quoted from President Clinton's "Forest Summit" held in Oregon, April 2, 1993.

32. Newton and Dillingham 1994: 14. Quoted from an article, "The Talk of the Town," in *The New Yorker*, June 29, 1992.

33. Morris 1984: 11.

34. Wilson 1990: 52–53.

3. The Transamazon Today

1. The Museu is the oldest research institute in the Amazon, set up in the 1870s by a Swiss botanist, Emilio Goeldi.

2. Moran 1993.

3. For their rationales, see their Ph.D. dissertations. Moran 1975; N. Smith 1976a.

4. N. Smith notes that the government changed the name of the *agrovila* to Castelo Branco in honor of the military president who took power after the 1964 coup. (N. Smith 1976a.)

5. *Seu* and *Dona* attached to the first name are respectful but familiar forms of address in Portuguese.

6. *Terra roxa estruturada*—translates literally as "structured purple earth," named for the color of its clay (to be discussed in Chapter 4).

7. *jabuticaba*

8. jackfruit

9. *abobora*

10. Peccaries are native to the region.

11. Frake 1961: 53–59.

12. Standards have been changing. When Moran studied the area, under no circumstances would a man enter the house of another man if the man were not home. By contrast, in 1989 women were surprised when I expressed uneasiness at their invitations into the house when their husbands were gone. Though men still demonstrated what seemed to me an inordinate fear of cuckoldry, boundaries between the sexes appear to be breaking down.

13. This was true in Belém too—the few times my roommate and I ate really tasty meals were when his sisters and female friends came over and did most of the cooking. They also showed me a thing or two about washing my clothes, once I'd swallowed my pride and accepted their help. (I had resisted help partly due to state-

ments like "That's crazy, you washing your clothes when we have so many women around.")

4. Castles in the Sand

1. Hecht and Cockburn 1989: 41–42.

2. Sanchez, Nicholaides, and Couto 1983: 108–109.

3. N. Smith 1982: 37.

4. Asia and Africa have their own limiting factors. Notably, low nutrient reserves in Africa are comparable to those in Latin America, and areas with steep slopes cover 35 percent of Asia vs. 7 percent of Latin America. (See Moran 1993 and Sanchez et al. 1982.)

5. N. Smith 1982: 44–45.

6. Hecht and Cockburn 1989: 37.

7. Simmons 1992: A6.

8. Ibid.

9. N. Smith 1982: 45. Smith cites his 1976 article, "Utilization of Game along Brazil's Transamazon Highway," on game yields and biomass.

10. Ibid., 44.

11. In his article "Does Swidden Ape the Jungle?" Beckerman is quick to point out that swidden methods are quite varied, and some are more sustainable than others. The diversity of the agricultural plot, he notes, in no way compares to the diversity of a rainforest. One or two subsistence crops, like manioc or corn, usually account for a large proportion of the area planted. (Beckerman 1983: 1–12.)

12. Geertz 1963: 16–20. Charles Wagley discussed an Amazonian swidden system in the context of *caboclo* farming in his *Amazon Town*. *Caboclos* drew their techniques and cultivars from both indigenous and European traditions.

13. Irvine 1989: 224.

14. Anderson 1989.

15. Balée 1989: 14.

16. Posey 1989. See also Posey, in Hecht and Cockburn 1989, Appendix B.

17. There are a few exceptions. Some colonists are descendants of recently acculturated Native Americans (acculturated in the past few generations) or former *caboclos*, Amazonian backwoodsmen and forest peoples. When I took a hike with a group through the forest, one man (whose grandparents had been born into a local forest tribe) demonstrated a markedly greater understanding of the ecosystem than his colonist compatriots who had migrated to the region from other parts of Brazil.

18. N. Smith 1982: 99–114.

19. N. Smith 1981: 759. Smith notes that yellow fever, which is endemic in certain monkey species of the region, never infected as many colonists as might have been expected. Only two colonists had contracted yellow fever and only one had

died of it by his 1978 study. By comparison, 1285 people were admitted to the Altamira and Marabá hospitals in 1973 alone for malaria and 26 died. As the rate of new colonization slowed, so did incidence of malaria. He attributes the low rate of yellow fever infection to the fact that "colonists clear forests during the dry season, when populations of the canopy vectors are probably at their lowest." Contrary to expectations, forested areas did not serve as reservoirs of disease waiting to be unleashed; people brought disease with them from populated areas.

20. N. Smith 1982: 101.

21. Lovejoy and Salati 1983: 215; Moran 1990: 25–26.

22. Hecht and Cockburn 1989: 41.

23. Even at the height of deforestation during the 1980s, Brazil's contribution of carbon dioxide and other greenhouse gasses was dwarfed by the output of the United States and other developed nations. Whenever we talk about global warming, I think it is healthy to remind ourselves of our own sins. Though the U.S. holds 5 percent of the world's population, it produces 22 percent of all carbon dioxide and consumes 25 percent of the world's energy. Brazilians are actually well aware of the disparities between greenhouse contributions and greenhouse blame—such statistics blanketed the popular press while I was there. (Elmer-Dewitt 1992.)

24. Quoted in Bingham 1990: 40.

25. Berkes et al. 1989: 91.

26. From discussion with Emilio Moran.

27. N. Smith 1982: 36.

28. Soil ecologists also describe soils according to sand and clay content. Pedro Sanchez uses the following four categories to classify Amazonian soils:

1. Acid, infertile soils (74.7 percent of Amazon Basin) A. Oxisols (i.e., *latosol amarelo muito pesado*, "very heavy yellow latosol"): 76–89 percent clay/ 5–15 percent sand. (Mixed soils.) B. Ultisols: 6–24 percent clay/54–80 percent sand. (Sandy soils.)
2. Poorly drained alluvial soils: 13.6 percent of Amazon Basin. Mollisols. Flood plain areas.
3. Moderately fertile, well-drained soils: 8.4 percent of Amazon. Alfisols (*terra roxa estruturada eutrófica*): 48–71 percent clay/15–34 percent sand.
4. Very infertile sandy soils: 3.3 percent of Amazon. Spodosols: 2–16 percent clay/76–89 percent sand. (Sandy soils.)

I find Sanchez's further breakdown helpful in that it describes general characteristics first, then gives percentages of sand and clay content. Though colonists' "good" soils—*terra roxa* and good mix—both contain significant amounts of nutrient rich clay, they are not necessarily well drained and may be acidic. (Sanchez, Nicholaides, and Couto 1983: 108.)

29. *Babaçu* palms may also indicate previous human occupation. In a 1992 survey of Transamazonian secondary growth, a team of researchers led by Emilio Moran reports that *babaçu* dominates repeatedly burned pasture lands. (Personal communication.) That colonists encounter *babaçu* in forests growing on particularly fertile soil might suggest that native people chose such fertile areas for their own agriculture. *Babaçu* growth could lead ethnoecologists and archaeologists to other anthropogenic forests and other areas occupied by agricultural settlements before the arrival of Europeans.

30. Moran noted the ability of local homesteaders (*caboclos*) to choose the best lots on the basis of vegetation cover in the early stages of colonization. (Moran 1989b: 183, fig. 3). Non-local settlers at the outset of colonization often chose their lots on the basis of the number of large trees a lot held, assuming that large trees indicated good soils. Non-locals were sorely mistaken. Unfortunately for the newcomers, large trees are often adapted to the worst soils in the Amazon. Their buttresses stretch out, spreading a broad but shallow root structure to capture nutrients that fall as debris from the canopy and to keep the tree from falling on thin soils. *Caboclos* consistently chose the more fertile soils; non-locals did not.

5. Frontier Agroeconomics

1. Moran 1981; N. Smith 1982: 62–92.

2. Moran 1981: 84.

3. N. Smith 1982: 68.

4. Ibid., 71.

5. Ibid., 64–71.

6. Mahar 1989.

7. N. Smith 1982: 77–87.

8. Some agronomic studies double count areas that are double-cropped in a year (Durham 1979: 31). For example, if one hectare produces a crop of corn, one of beans, and one of manioc in a single year, it would be counted as three hectares when compiling the statistics. This method will not be employed here, though colonists do double- and triple-crop areas. If double-cropping were counted, the conclusions on cropping patterns made later in this chapter would become even more striking.

Labor time on pasture was calculated from fencing five hectares and dividing by five for man-days/ha. This number gets smaller if pasture does not require so much fencing, which is the case on larger ranches. Fencing helps in pasture rotation, which increases production and prolongs the productive life of the pasture when done properly.

9. Figures are calculated at the frontier's going rate of NCr$10/man-day

(U.S.$2.50/man-day). Estimates taken from interview at EMATER, August 8, 1989.

10. Exceptions to this were the CIRA-PACAL sugar growers around Km. 92.

11. Interview with agricultural technician at CEPLAC in Médicilandia, August 3, 1989.

12. N. Smith 1982: 80.

13. Interview with CEPLAC director in Altamira, August 8, 1989.

14. N. Smith, personal communication.

15. At Tomé-Açu in eastern Pará, diseased plants were pulled up and burned, then a moratorium on new plants was declared in the region for five years—unusually strong measures for a crop disease!

16. N. Smith 1982: 82.

17. Interviews with EMATER and EMBRAPA, July 18, 1989.

18. Interview with CEPLAC director, August 8, 1989.

19. Davis 1978; Mahar 1979; Hecht and Cockburn 1989.

20. Moran 1981: 143–150.

21. For land appreciation see Mahar 1989. For tax holidays see Hecht and Cockburn 1989: 53. Uhl was working for a government research agency in Belém while I was there, and Moran told me of his work, but I have not found his results published. Agricultural technicians working for both EMBRAPA and EMATER reported that cattle were either marginal or unprofitable as an investment. Nigel Smith disputes these claims, saying cattle can be marginally profitable and sustainable even for small holders.

22. Wilson 1990: 59.

23. Hecht and Cockburn 1989: 107.

24. Brazil does not take part in the "Burger King Connection"—the importation of rainforest beef to the United States. South American beef is barred from the U.S. market because it has not been certified as free of the *aftosa* virus (Williams 1986: 85). The United States does obtain cheap beef from Central America. The United States government encouraged export-driven agriculture in Central America with preferential treatment in trade. Consequently, Central America's rainforests have disappeared much more rapidly than Brazil's since the 1950s.

25. Hecht and Cockburn state that only one cowboy is needed for every 3,600 acres cleared on large *glebas*. This quite probably does not include the cost of continued weeding and burning to maintain the pasture, but the figure is still astonishing (Hecht and Cockburn 1989: 153).

26. Hecht and Cockburn 1989: 150.

27. Fearnside's estimates are not nearly as favorable, at up to three head per hectare.

28. N. Smith, personal communication, October 15, 1992.

29. UNESCO 1979.

30. Wilson 1989: 59. Christopher Uhl has worked on this, but I have not found his findings in print.

31. I heard this everywhere I went, including during interviews with farmers at my primary site and at Kilometer 90 and with agronomists from São Paulo.

32. N. Smith 1982: 51–52.

33. Lovejoy and Salati 1983: 217.

34. Posey 1983: 234.

35. For a description of surface and substrata soil composition along the Transamazon, see N. Smith, 1982: 38–39; Falesi, 1972.

36. Smith 1982: 80, 82.

37. Figure 5.5 does not include second growth and therefore should not be used to measure the mean amount of land deforested.

38. Moran 1981: 91–96.

39. Ibid., 225.

40. Ibid., 90–93. I refrain from using Moran's social classification system; farmers I have previously referred to as "entrepreneurial" do not necessarily conform to his definitions and categories.

41. In two cases, families of workers lived on what might be considered secondary lots; they rented the lots. In such cases, the secondary lot may as well have been owned by the family working the lot, as that family took most of the profits and were paid for any improvements made on the lot during their tenure. One case was the only lot of an absentee owner who lived in Altamira. I counted this as a primary lot because it was the owner's only lot, and he and his family were carefully overseeing the operation and planned to occupy the lot when the economic situation for agriculture improved. The surrounding lots were owned and worked by other members of his family. The other case I counted as secondary, even though it had three families of workers living on it. The owner allowed them to put half the lot under agriculture for their own profit, but the other half was pasture. The owner had six lots total, four of which were entirely (all 100 hectares) pasture. He put the one on which he lived entirely under crops. All six of his lots were of *terra roxa*. I counted the workers' lot as "secondary" in order to be consistent, although it was used as if it were the primary lot of the workers. Had I not counted this as a secondary lot, the mean hectares of agriculture on secondary lots would have been virtually zero.

42. Durham 1979: 52.

43. He adds that we should let ruminants eat *what* people can't as well. Grain-fed beef wastes precious resources. Think of all the energy that goes into feeding a cow with grain. One not only feeds the cow but also dams and then drains the river, fills the tractor and pollutes the air, poisons the insects, and kills the "weeds" that heartier ruminants could eat.

6. Considering a Second Redistribution

1. N. Smith 1982: 23.
2. N. Smith, personal communication, October 15, 1992.
3. Dominique Irvine, personal communication, Nov. 1990.
4. Moran 1981: 78–96 and 1989b; Foweraker 1981; Nelson 1973.
5. N. Smith 1982.
6. Balée 1989: 9.
7. N. Smith 1982: 45.
8. According to the director of the lumber mill at the CIRA-PACAL project (Km. 92), most Amazonian logging operations have stridently resisted any move toward government-mandated reforestation programs.
9. Note that simple calculations put the projected cost of reforestation at $3,000 per hectare. The cost of deforestation runs about $60 to $70 for 22 man-days of labor per hectare. (From "Brazil Approves Plan for Amazon Reforesting" 1990.) Keep in mind the reforestation project is likely to be only partially successful and will hardly replace the biodiverse primary rainforests. According to Catherine Caufield, large clear-cut areas have never been successfully reforested in the humid tropics (Caufield 1984).
10. The PACAL lumber mill received $679 per cubic meter of cut mahogany.

7. The Rise of Collective Action

1. N. Smith 1982; Moran 1981; Bunker 1985; Dias and Castro 1986; Nelson 1973.
2. In the process of increasing cacao production, the Ivory Coast suffered one of the highest deforestation rates in the world.
3. From interviews with CEPLAC in Médicilandia and Altamira.
4. The Populist movement of the 1880s and 1890s in the United States similarly gained momentum (beginning in Texas and spreading throughout the South and the West) due to its ability to establish higher prices for small farmers through collective bargaining with distributors and to secure credit with the banks (Goodwyn 1978: 20–54). Parallels between the development of Brazilian colonist associations and grassroots organizations and the development of populism in the United States are striking.
5. *Capoeira* is the secondary growth after a forest is cut down. It grows more rapidly on fertile soils than infertile and often reaches a height of twenty feet within two or three years.
6. Moran 1981: 226.
7. For more schooling, children had to go to Altamira and live with relatives or

friends. A few of the older (and by now wealthier) colonists could support their children in Altamira and had friends there in whose houses students could stay.

8. If it had been an emergency, one of the neighbors with a car would have driven the baby.

9. An *agrópolis* is a large *agrovila* and administrative center in the INCRA *urbanismo-rural* scheme.

10. Bunker 1985: 201–202.

11. Ibid., 206.

12. N. Smith 1982: 88–92.

13. Bunker 1985: 214–215.

14. N. Smith 1982: 77.

15. Bunker 1985: 213.

16. Ibid., and interviews with colonists.

17. N. Smith 1982: 78.

18. The Arara had hostile dealings with colonists and the government ever since the road was cut in 1970. The Arara killed three workers on a government-sponsored geological survey in 1976. A settler who wandered into Arara lands was killed a year later. In 1979, two FUNAI workers were wounded while trying to contact the tribe. Smith reports, "The FUNAI workers were evacuated by helicopter to Altamira with several arrows protruding from their bodies." (N. Smith 1982: 90–91.) In the mid-1980s, twenty-six members of this tribe wandered into the colonized zone from the north side of the highway badly in need of medical attention. They were reunited with the rest of their tribe on the south side of the highway, along the Xingu. The tribe had been separated when the highway was built. Fewer than 100 members survived contact. I spoke with no one who really knew how many had lived in the region before settlers came. (From interview with FUNAI in Altamira.)

19. Caufield 1984: 167.

20. Bunker 1985: 216.

21. Nelson 1973: 265.

22. Personal communication, August 8, 1989.

23. For a comparison of the efficacy of small groups and the need for member participation, see the landmark study *The Logic of Collective Action* by Mancur Olson, 1980: 53–57.

24. Freire 1970, from Wilber, ed., 1988: 547.

25. Hecht and Cockburn 1989: 169.

26. This statement oversimplifies a complex history. Drawing comparisons between Central American land struggles and those of Brazil would be beyond the scope of this book. For some discussion of land invasions and land reform in the context of peasants and export agriculture, see Williams 1986.

8. The Future for Small Farmers in Amazonia

1. Flaherty et al. 1992, S. V. "Phylloxera."
2. Wilson 1990: 58; Wilson 1992: 285.
3. Lovejoy, quoted in Elmer-Dewitt 1992: 45.
4. Dominique Irvine, personal communication, December 1990.
5. Personal communication from Susanna Hecht on April 12, 1991.
6. Reported by National Public Radio on March 15, 1993.

GLOSSARY

Portuguese Words Used in the Text

açaí (*Euterpe oleracea*):   a pungent purple fruit that makes a tasty drink; heart of palm comes from the heart of *açaí* palm trees.

agrópolis: a large *agrovila* and regional administrative headquarters for INCRA.

agrovila: government-built colonization town.

barcasa: a cement slab (small) or wooden structure with removable, rolling roof used to lay out and dry agricultural products (coffee, pepper, cacao) in the sun.

beneficiado: improved.

caboclo: a term describing Brazil's equivalent to "backwoodsman." Can carry a pejorative connotation. City people call "country bumpkins" *caboclos*, country bumpkins call Amazonian riverine (forest) people *caboclos*, and they in turn refer to the Indians as *caboclos*. Some indigenous tribes refer to non-indigenous peoples as "termite people." No one ever told me the term for nosy American ecological anthropologists.

capoeira: second forest growth.

casa de farinha: literally a "farinha house" where manioc is processed into *farinha*, a nutritious flour. The *casa de farinha* includes an oven, a grater, a pit for fermentation, a manual compressor, and sometimes a motor for grating.

cigarrinha: a small grasshopper that destroys rice and grass from underground.

favelas: slums on the hills of Rio de Janeiro.

gaucho: cowboy.

glebas: large farms.

glebistas: owners of these large farms.

grilheros: land grabbers, or large holders who appropriate lands from others by force or by manipulation of government surveyors.

Junina: festival during the month of June.

lavoura branca: staple crops of rice, corn, beans, and manioc.

lavoura definitiva: specialized, perennial crops.

manioc: a tuber-root native to the Amazon and a primary source of calories for many native peoples as well as colonists.

mata de cipó: liana (vine) forests, a type of upland forest with an uneven and relatively low canopy, probably the result of long-term human occupation.

Não têm condições: "They do not have the means."

onça (Panthera onça): jaguar.

Ordem e Progresso: Order and Progress (slogan written across Brazilian flag).

reunião: a meeting or get-together.

sem terras: the landless.

terra firme: uplands.

travessão: side road.

trilhadeira: threshing machine.

urbanismo-rural: rural urbanism.

urucú (Bixa orelana): a plant native to Amazonia, the seeds of which make a bright red dye for food or body paint.

várzea: the floodplains of rivers. In the Amazon basin they are generally fertile because their soils are replenished annually from the Andes (and now from deforested and unprotected lands) and considered ideal for some kinds of agriculture.

vassoura de bruxa (Crine perniciosa): "witch's broom," a fungus that attacks cacao in the Amazon.

SOURCES

Abbey, Edward. 1968. *Desert Solitaire: A Season in the Wilderness*. New York: McGraw-Hill.

Adams, Richard N. 1973. *Energy and Structure*. Austin: University of Texas Press.

Alcorn, J. B. 1984. *Huastec Mayan Ethnobotany*. Austin: University of Texas Press.

Almeida, Anna Luiza Osorio de. 1992. *The Colonization of the Amazon*. Austin: University of Texas Press.

"Amazônia: Onde Está a Verdade?" 1989. *Veja, Edição Especial* 22(1): 60–109.

Anderson, Anthony. 1989. "Forest Management on the Amazonian *Várzea*." Lecture given on June 29 at the Museu Paraense Emilio Goeldi, Belém, Brazil.

Ayensu, Edward S. 1980. *The Life and Mysteries of the Jungle*. New York: Crescent Books.

Baer, Werner. 1979. *The Brazilian Economy: Its Growth and Development*. Columbus, Ohio: Grid Publishing Co.

Balée, William. 1989. "The Culture of Amazonian Forests." New York Botanical Garden, Institute of Economic Botany, *Advances in Economic Botany* 7: 1–21.

Beckerman, Stephan. 1983. "Does the Swidden Ape the Jungle?" *Human Ecology* 11(1): 1–12.

Berkes, F., et al. 1989. "The Benefits of the Commons." *Nature* 340: 91–93.

Bingham, Sam. 1990. "Rolling Back the Desert." *World Monitor (Christian Science Monitor Monthly)*, September, pp. 34–40.

"Brazil Approves Plan for Amazon Reforesting." 1990. *San Francisco Chronicle*, December 20.

Brooke, James. 1989. "Rain and Fires, but Mostly Rain, Slow Burning of Amazon Forest in Brazil." *New York Times*, September 17.

———. 1993. "In Brazil, Too, Withered Land Cries for Rain." *New York Times*, April 8.

Brown, L. R. 1978. *The Twenty-Ninth Day*. New York: Norton.

Bunker, Stephen G. 1985. *Underdeveloping the Amazon: Extraction, Unequal Exchange, and the Failure of the Modern State*. Chicago: University of Illinois Press.

Burns, E. Bradford. 1980. *A History of Brazil*. New York: Columbia University Press.

Cardoso, Fernando Henrique. 1973. "Associated Dependent Development: Theoretical and Practical Implications." In *Authoritarian Brazil: Origins, Policies and Future*, edited by Alfred Stepan, pp. 142–178. New Haven: Yale University Press.

Cardoso, Fernando Henrique, and Geraldo Müller. 1977. *Amazônia: Expansão do Capitalismo*. São Paulo: Editora Brasiliense.

Caufield, Catherine. 1984. *In the Rainforest*. Chicago: University of Chicago Press.

Cehelsky, Marta. 1979. *Land Reform in Brazil: The Management of Social Change*. Boulder: Westview Press.

Coelho, João Gilberto Lucas, and Antonio Carlos Montes de Oliveira. 1989. *A Nova Constituição: Avaliação de Texto e Perfil dos Constituintes*. Rio de Janeiro: Editora Revan.

Conklin, Harold C. 1954. "An Ethnoecological Approach to Shifting Agriculture." *Transactions of the New York Academy of Sciences* 17(2): 133–142.

Contini, Emilio. 1976. "A Colonização na Transamazônica." M.A. thesis, Rio de Janeiro, Fundação Getúlio Vargas.

Cronon, William. 1983. *Changes in the Land: Indians, Colonists, and the Ecology of New England*. New York: Hill and Wang.

Davis, Shelton H. 1978. *Victims of the Miracle*. New York: Cambridge University Press.

Dias, Guilherme Leite da Silva, and Manoel Cabral de Castro. 1986. *A Colonização Oficial no Brasil: Erros e Acertos na Fronteira Agrícola*. São Paulo: Instituto de Pesquisas Econômicas.

Durham, William. 1979. *Scarcity and Survival in Central America: Ecological Origins of the Soccer War*. Stanford: Stanford University Press.

Eccles, W. J. 1982. *The Canadian Frontier 1534–1760*. Albuquerque: University of New Mexico Press.

Elmer-Dewitt, Philip. 1992. "Rich vs. Poor." *Time Magazine*, June 1, pp. 44–58.

Falesi, I. 1972. "Solos da Rodovia Transamazônica." *Boletim Técnico do Instituto de Pesquisa Agropecuária do Norte* 55: 1–196.

Fearnside, Phillip M. 1978. *Estimation of Human Carrying Capacity for Human Populations in a Part of the Transamazon Colonization Area of Brazil*. Ph.D. dissertation, University of Michigan. Ann Arbor: University Microfilms International.

———. 1983. "Development Alternatives in Brazilian Amazon: An Ecological Analysis." *Interciencia* 8(2): 65–78.

———. 1986a. "Agricultural Plans for Brazil's Grande Carajas Program: Lost Opportunity for Sustainable Local Development." *World Development*, March, pp. 371–412.

———. 1986b. *Human Carrying Capacity of the Brazilian Amazon*. New York: Columbia University Press.

Flaherty, Donald L., et al. 1992. *Grape Pest Management*, 2d ed. Oakland: Agriculture and Natural Resources Publications, no. 3343.

Foweraker, Joe. 1981. *The Struggle for Land.* New York: Cambridge University Press.

Frake, Charles. 1961. "Cultural Ecology and Ethnography." *American Anthropologist* 64(1), pt. 1: 53–59.

Freire, Paulo. 1970. *Pedagogy of the Oppressed.* Reprinted in *The Political Economy of Development and Underdevelopment*, edited by Charles K. Wilber, 1988, pp. 540–559. New York: Random House.

Gates, Paul. 1974. "Research in the History of the Public Lands." *Agricultural History* 48: 31–50.

Geertz, Clifford. 1963. *Agricultural Involution: The Processes of Ecological Change in Indonesia.* Berkeley: University of California Press.

Goodland, R. J. A., and H. S. Irwin. 1975. *Amazon Jungle: Green Hell to Red Desert?* Amsterdam: Elsevier.

Goodwyn, Lawrence. 1978. *The Populist Moment: A Short History of the Agrarian Revolt in America.* New York: Oxford University Press.

Gould, Stephen J. 1987. *Time's Arrow, Time's Cycle: Myth and Metaphor in the Discovery of Geological Time.* Cambridge: Harvard University Press.

Hall, Anthony L. 1986. "More of the Same in the Brazilian Amazon: A Comment on Fearnside." *World Development*, March, pp. 413–416.

———. 1989. *Developing Amazônia.* Manchester: Manchester University Press.

Hample, Stuart, and Eric Marshall. 1991. *Children's Letters to God: The New Collection.* New York: Workman Publishing.

Hardin, Garrett. 1968. "The Tragedy of the Commons." *Science* 162: 1243–1248.

Hecht, Susanna, and Alexander Cockburn. 1989. *The Fate of the Forest: Developers, Destroyers, and Defenders of the Amazon.* New York: Verso.

INCRA. 1972. *Colonização da Amazônia: Política de Integracão Nacional.* Brasília: Government Publication.

Irvine, Dominique. 1989. "Succession Management and Resource Distribution in an Amazonian Rain Forest." New York Botanical Garden, Institute of Economic Botany, *Advances in Economic Botany* 7: 223–237.

Johnson, Allen. 1974. "Ethnoecology and Planting Practices in a Swidden Agricultural System." *American Ethnologist* 1: 87–101.

Kemper, Robert V. 1977. *Migration and Adaptation: Tzintzuntzan Peasants in Mexico City.* Beverly Hills: Sage Publications.

Kuznets, Simon. 1955. "Economic Growth and Income Inequality." *American Economic Review* 45, no. 1 (March): 1–28.

———. 1984. "Economic Growth and Income Inequality." In *The Gap between Rich and Poor: Contending Perspectives on Development*, edited by Mitchell A. Seligson, pp. 25–37. Boulder, Colo.: Westview Press.

Linden, Eugene. 1992. "Rio's Legacy." *Time Magazine*, June 22, pp. 44–45.

Locke, John. 1980. *Second Treatise on Government*. Edited by C. B. MacPhearson. Indianapolis: Hackett Publishing Company, Inc.

Lovejoy, Thomas E., and Eneas Salati. 1983. "Precipitating Change in Amazônia." In *The Dilemma of Amazonian Development*, edited by Emilio F. Moran, pp. 211–220. Boulder: Westview Press.

Mahar, Dennis J. 1979. *Development Policy in Brazil: A Study of Amazônia*. New York: Praeger Publishers.

———. 1983. "Development of the Brazilian Amazon: Prospects for the 1980's." In *The Dilemma of Amazonian Development*, edited by Emilio F. Moran, pp. 319–334. Boulder: Westview Press.

———. 1989. *Government Policy and Deforestation*. Washington, D.C.: World Bank.

McIntyre, Loren. 1991. *Amazonia*. Tokyo: Sierra Club Books.

"The Message of the Trees." 1993. *New York Times*, Editorial, April 3.

Meyers, Norman. 1984. *The Primary Source: Tropical Forests and Our Future*. New York: W. W. Norton and Co.

Moran, Emilio F. 1973–1974. Field Notes: Soil Samples Taken on Side Roads and along the Transamazon Highway. (Personal communication.)

———. 1975. *Pioneer Farmers of the Transamazon Highway: Adaptation and Agricultural Production in the Lowland Tropics*. Ph.D. dissertation, University of Florida.

———. 1978. "Strategies for Survival: Resource Use along the Transamazon Highway." In *Changing Agricultural Systems in Latin America*, pp. 49–75. Studies in Third World Societies, Publication 7. Williamsburg, Va.: College of William and Mary, Dept. of Anthropology.

———. 1981. *Developing the Amazon*. Bloomington: Indiana University Press.

———. 1983. "Growth without Development: Past and Present Development Efforts in Amazônia." In *The Dilemma of Amazonian Development*, edited by Emilio F. Moran, pp. 3–24. Boulder: Westview Press.

———. 1984. "Social Reproduction in Agricultural Frontiers." In *Production and Autonomy: Anthropological Studies and Critiques of Development*, edited by John Bowen and John Bennett, pp. 199–212. Boulder: Westview Press.

———. 1987a. "A Comparative Analysis of the Amazonian and the U.S. Frontiers." Paper given October 1 at Indiana University Economic History Workshop.

———. 1987b. "Monitoring Fertility Degradation of Agricultural Lands in the Lowland Tropics." In *Lands at Risk in the Third World: Local-Level Perspectives*, edited by Peter D. Little and Michael M. Horowitz. Boulder: Westview Press.

———. 1988. "Following the Amazonian Highways." In *People of the Tropical Rainforest*, edited by Julie Denslow and Christine Padoch, pp. 155–162. Berkeley: University of California Press.

———. 1989a. "Adaptation and Maladaptation in Newly Settled Areas." In *The*

• Sources •

Human Ecology of Tropical Land Settlement in Latin America, edited by Debra A. Schumann and William L. Partridge. San Francisco: Westview Press.

———. 1989b. "Government-Directed Settlement in the 1970s: An Assessment of Transamazon Highway Colonization." In *The Human Ecology of Tropical Land Settlement in Latin America*, edited by Debra A. Schumann and William L. Partridge. San Francisco: Westview Press.

———. 1989c. "Models of Native Folk Adaptation in the Amazon." New York Botanical Garden, Institute of Economic Botany, *Advances in Economic Botany* 7: 22–29.

———. 1990. *A Ecologia Human das Populações da Amazônia*. Petrópolis, Rio de Janeiro, Editora Vozes.

———. 1993. *Through Amazonian Eyes: The Human Ecology of Amazonian Populations*. Iowa City: University of Iowa Press.

Moran, Emilio F., ed. 1983. *The Dilemma of Amazonian Development*. Boulder: Westview Press.

Morris, Richard. 1984. *Time's Arrow*. New York: Simon and Schuster.

Motta, Roberto, ed. 1985. *A Amazônia em Questão: Anais do IV Encontro Inter-Regional de Cientistas Sociais do Brasil*. Recife: Editora Massangana.

Nelson, Michael. 1973. *The Development of Tropical Lands: Policy Issues in Latin America*. Baltimore: John Hopkins University Press.

Neto, F. 1989. *National and Global Dimensions of Regional Development Planning: A Case-Study of Brazilian Amazônia*. Ph.D. thesis, London School of Economics and Political Science, University of London.

Netting, Robert M. 1981. *Balancing on an Alp: Ecological Change and Continuity in a Swiss Mountain Community*. New York: Cambridge University Press.

Newman, Arnold. 1990. *Tropical Rainforests*. New York: Facts on File, Inc.

Newton, Lisa, and Catherine Dillingham. In press. *Watersheds: Classic Cases in Environmental Ethics*. (Scheduled to be published in 1994 by Wadsworth Publishing Company, Belmont, Calif.)

Oliveira, Ariovaldo Umbelino de. 1988. *Integrar Para Não Entregar: Políticas Públicas e Amazônia*. Brasilia: n. p.

Olson, Mancur. 1980. *The Logic of Collective Action*. Cambridge, Mass.: Harvard University Press.

Oltman, David. 1993. "Soil Savers." *California Farmer*, April.

Posey, Daryl A. 1983. "Indigenous Ecological Knowledge and Development of the Amazon." In *The Dilemma of Amazonian Development*, edited by Emilio F. Moran, pp. 225–258. Boulder: Westview Press.

———. 1989. "Forest Management by Kayapô." Lecture given on June 29 at the Museu Paraense Emilio Goeldi, Belém, Brazil.

Prance, Gillian T., and Thomas Lovejoy, eds. 1985. *Amazônia*. New York: Pergamon Press.

Rappaport, Roy A. 1984. *Pigs for the Ancestors: Ritual in the Ecology of a New Guinea People*. New Haven: Yale University Press.

Rattner, Henrique, and Olivier Udry. 1987. *Colonização na Fronteira Amazônica: Expansão e Conflitos*. São Paulo: Instituto de Pesquisas Econômicas.

Reisner, Marc. 1987. *Cadillac Desert: The American West and Its Disappearing Water*. New York: Penguin Group.

Roett, Riordan. 1972. *Brazil: Politics in a Patrimonial Society*. Boston: Little, Brown and Company.

Roosevelt, A. 1989. "Resource Management in Amazônia before the Conquest: Beyond Ethnographic Projections." New York Botanical Garden, Institute of Economic Botany, *Advances in Economic Botany* 7: 30–62.

SAIIC (South and Mesoamerican Indian Information Center). 1987. *SAIIC Newsletter* 3(3). Oakland: South and Meso-American Indian Information Center.

———. 1988. *SAIIC Newsletter* 4(1). Oakland: South and Meso-American Indian Information Center.

———. 1989. *SAIIC Newsletter* 4(2 & 3). Oakland: South and Meso-American Indian Information Center.

Sanchez, Pedro A. 1976. *Properties and Management of Soils in the Tropics*. New York: Wiley-Interscience.

Sanchez, P. A., and J. Benites. 1987. "Low-input Cropping for Acid Soils of the Humid Tropics." *Science* 238: 1521–1527.

Sanchez, P. A., et al. 1982. "Amazon Basin Soils: Management for Continuous Crop Production." *Science* 216: 821–827.

Sanchez, P. A., J. J. Nicholaides III, and A. J. Couto. 1983. "Crop Production Systems in the Amazon Basin." In *The Dilemma of Amazonian Development*, edited by Emilio F. Moran, pp. 101–154. Boulder: Westview Press.

Schmink, M., and C. H. Woods, eds. 1985. *Frontier Expansion in Amazônia*. Gainesville: University of Florida Press.

Schuh, G. Edward. 1970. *The Agricultural Development of Brazil*. New York: Praeger.

SEPLAN (Secretaria de Planejamento). 1984. *Programa Institucional de Cooperativismo*. Brasília: Conselho Nacional de Desenvolvimento Científico e Technológico (CNPq).

Shoumatoff, Alex. 1990. *The World Is Burning*. Boston: Little, Brown and Company.

Simmons, Marlise. 1992. "Winds Toss Africa's Soil, Feeding Lands Far Away." *New York Times*, October 29.

Sindicato dos Trabalhadores Rurais de Médicilândia, Pará. 1988. "Relatório do Acampamento dos Posseiros." (Re labor action.) Mimeo.

———. 1989. "Nota de Esclarecimento." (Re invasion of Indian lands.) Mimeo.

Skidmore, Thomas E., and Peter H. Smith. 1984. *Modern Latin America*. New York: Oxford University Press.

Smith, Bradford P. 1990. *Large Animal Internal Medicine*. St. Louis: C. V. Mosby.

Smith, Nigel J. H. 1976a. *Transamazon Highway: A Cultural Ecological Analysis of Settlement in the Lowland Tropics*. Ph.D. dissertation, Department of Geography, University of California, Berkeley.

———. 1976b. "Utilization of Game along Brazil's Transamazon Highway." *Acta Amazonica* 6(4): 455–466.

———. 1981. "Colonization Lessons from a Tropical Forest." *Science* 214 (4522): 755–761.

———. 1982. *Rainforest Corridors*. Berkeley: University of California Press.

Stepan, Alfred, ed. 1973. *Authoritarian Brazil: Origins, Policies, and Future*. New Haven: Yale University Press.

Stevens, William K. 1990. "Research in 'Virgin' Amazon Uncovers Complex Farming." *New York Times*, April 3.

Steward, Julian. 1972. *Theory of Culture Change: The Methodology of Multilinear Evolution*. Chicago: University of Illinois Press.

Sturtevant, William. 1964. "Studies in Ethnoscience." *American Anthropologist* 66(3), pt. 2: 99–131.

Switkes, Glenn. 1988. "World Bank Backs the Drowning of Amazônia." *World Rivers Review*, October, pp. 1, 5–10.

Tonucci, Padre Paulo M., org. 1981. *Igreja e Problemas da Terra*. Petrópolis: Editora Vozes.

Uhl, Christopher. 1989. "Disturbance and Regeneration in Amazonia." *Ecologist* 19(6).

UNESCO. 1979. *Man and the Humid Tropics*. Paris: UNESCO. Slides.

Veblen, Thorstein. 1953. *The Theory of the Leisure Class*. Ontario: NAL Penguin, Inc.

Wagley, Charles. 1964. *Amazon Town: A Study of Man in the Tropics*. New York: Alfred A. Knopf, First Borzoi Edition.

———. 1978. *Welcome of Tears: The Tapirape Indians of Central Brazil*. New York: Oxford University Press.

Wilber, Charles K., ed. 1988. *The Political Economy of Development and Underdevelopment*. New York: Random House.

Williams, Robert G. 1986. *Export Agriculture and the Crisis in Central America*. Chapel Hill: University of North Carolina Press.

Wilson, Edward O. 1990. "Threats to Biodiversity." In *Managing Planet Earth: Readings from Scientific American*, pp. 49–59. New York: W. H. Freeman and Co.

———. 1992. *The Diversity of Life*. Cambridge: Harvard University Press.

INDEX

açaí, 59, 149
Acre, state of, 141
adaptation. *See* agroforestry: indigenous techniques; colonists: adaptation strategies of; forest peoples: use
  of forest resources; Native Americans: use of resources; soils: distribution and effects on agriculture of
Africa, 54–55, 57, 106, 156
aftosa virus, 159n
agrarian reform. *See* land: expropriation and redistribution; land: pressures for further redistribution of;
  land: social distribution of
agriculture: annuals, 13, 39–40; export,
  118–121; government supports for,
  71–75, 77–80, 127–136; history of,
  in Brazil, 11; impact of, on ecosystem, 60–66; market influences on,
  71, 75, 77, 79, 80–86, 88, 96,
  118–121, 150–151; maximizing
  yields of, 74, 77, 90–93; mechanization of, 49–50, 73–75, 127–136;
  mixed cropping, 76–77; pests and
  diseases of, 40, 60–61, 73–74,
  80–88, 91–92, 96, 147–148; prices
  in, 46–47; recuperating degraded
  areas in, 90–92; soil distribution as
  indicator for, 92–101; along Trans-

amazon, 12–14, 16. *See also* agroforestry; annual crops; cacao; cattle
  ranching; exports; pasture; pepper;
  perennial crops; rice; soils: distribution and effects on agriculture of;
  sugarcane; swidden agriculture;
  viticulture
agroforestry, 7, 18–19, 22–25, 77,
  111–112, 146–151; indigenous
  techniques of, 58–60. *See also* agriculture: history in Brazil; agriculture:
  along Transamazon; Brazil nuts;
  cacao; rubber
agronomistas, 50
agrovilas, 13, 29–32, 40, 44, 121,
  124–126
Alaska, 104–106
Altamira, 2, 3, 6, 28–30, 63, 120, 141
Amapá, Brazil, 27
Amazonia, 3. *See also* colonization,
  Amazonian; ecosystem; Transamazon Highway
annual crops (*lavoura branca*), 71–77,
  135–136
Anopheles darlingi. *See* mosquitoes
ants. *See* leaf-cutter ants
Arara (tribe), 140–141, 162n
Asia, 53–54, 156
associations, agricultural, 120–121

described, 54–69; protection of, 22–25, 65, 107–114, 131–134, 146–151. *See also* forest; soils
Ecuador, 150
Eduardo (truck driver), 2–3, 115–118
education, 13, 44, 46, 117, 126, 134; colonists' construction of schools, 8, 121, 123–125; technical assistance, 70–71, 77
EMATER, x, 47, 96
EMBRAPA, x, 44, 47
empates, 141–142
Endangered Species Act (U.S.), 22–23
entrepreneurialism, 41–42, 44, 75, 79
environment. *See* ecosystem
equilibrium, 57–58
erosion. *See* soils: erosion of
ethnoecology, 26, 28–29, 39–43, 45–51
evapotranspiration. *See* hydrology
evolution, 25
exports: historical, 11; model for growth, 11–16, 77–78. *See also* agriculture: export; perennial crops
expropriation, 10, 87. *See also* land use
extinction, xiv, 23–25
extractive reserves, 108–109
extractivism, 15, 38–39, 59, 91, 108–109

favelas, 12
fertilizers, 90–91
fire, 58–59, 60, 65
fish, 131
forest: canopy, 32, 55–56; described, 32–33, 154n; human impact on, 58–66; preservation of, 107–114; secondary growth, 65, 90, 161n; types (mature upland, *mata de cipó*), 52–58
forest management. *See* agroforestry

forest peoples: ix; history of, 15, 27; perspectives on development of, 19–20; and prospects for reserves, 108–109; use of forest resources by, 18–19, 58–60, 69, 156
forest products, 146–151; collection of, 5, 89; described, 28; sale of, xiv, 23–25
France, 21, 148–149
Freire, Paulo, 141
frontier: see Amazonia; United States: western frontier; development
fruits: *abobora*, coconut, *urucú* (also *corrante* or *Bixa orelana*), *jabuticaba*, *jáca*, described, 37. *See also açaí*; agriculture: market influences on; agroforestry; cacao: advantage of tree crops and agroforestry; perennial crops: *taperebá*
FUNAI, 162n
fungicides: chemical, 85; natural, 91
FUNRURAL, x, 120
Fusarium s. piperi, 84–85

gap dynamics, 56–58. *See also* forest: canopy
garimpo, 44. See also mining
gender, 45–46, 48, 155–156n
geologic time, 23–25, 63–65
glebas, 16
glebistas, 16, 42, 104, 110. *See also* large farmers
global warming, 19, 61–65, 157
Goodland, Robert, 4–5
good mix. *See* soils: distribution and effects on; soils: heterogeneity of
government: agricultural support and subsidies by, 13, 71–75, 77–80, 96; cooperatives, 126–137. *See also* agriculture: government supports for; CEPLAC; CIRA; cooperatives; development: government's role in;